DRAWING A CROWD

DRAWING A CROWD

BILL GALLO'S GREATEST SPORTS MOMENTS

Bill Gallo
with Phil Cornell

 JONATHAN DAVID PUBLISHERS, INC.
Middle Village, New York 11379

DRAWING A CROWD
Bill Gallo's Greatest Sports Moments

Copyright © 2000
by
Bill Gallo and Phil Cornell

Address all inquiries to:

Jonathan David Publishers, Inc.
68-22 Eliot Avenue
Middle Village, New York 11379

www.jdbooks.com

2 4 6 8 10 9 7 5 3 1

Library of Congress Cataloging-in-Publication Data

Gallo, Bill
Drawing a crowd : Bill Gallo's greatest sports moments / by Bill Gallo with Phil Cornell.
   p. cm.
ISBN 0-8246-0421-0
1. Sports—Caricatures and cartoons. 2. American wit and humor, Pictorial. I. Title: Bill Gallo's greatest sports moments. II. Cornell, Phil. III. Title.

NC1429. G195 A4 2000
796'. 022'2—dc21
                            99-088280
                            CIP

Designed and composed by John Reinhardt Book Design

Printed in the United States of America

To my wife, Dolores

CONTENTS

ACKNOWLEDGMENTS

Drawing and writing are solitary pursuits—particularly when a deadline looms—but the creation of a book is a team effort, dependent on the belief and support of many.

In the early stages of this project, when words of encouragement were like drops of rain on a seedling, numerous book editors and publishers extended advice and good wishes, for no other reason than to see a worthy idea in print. The folks at Jonathan David Publishers allowed it to actually happen, and our thanks go to Alfred J. Kolatch, Fiorella de Lima, Marvin Sekler, and others there who fostered a congenial and productive relationship. In particular, David Kolatch at Jonathan David was our editorial linchpin, carefully coordinating countless details and regularly exhorting us to achieve the best outcome possible. His tireless enthusiasm, guidance and concern for quality were crucial to the final result.

A book such as this one depends on the visual impact of each page, and book designer John Reinhardt showcased these drawings patiently and skillfully.

At the *Daily News*, Harold Evans and John Campi were solidly in our corner from the outset and aided us with their invaluable skills and vast experience in publishing and promotion respectively. They have our sincerest thanks. The paper's crack library personnel, an ally to any reporter or editor in a pinch, came through for us repeatedly during our research missions. We salute chief librarian Faigi Rosenthal and her staff: Scott Browne, Jimmy Converso, Peter Edelman, Dawn Jackson, Ellen Locker, Alain Delaqueriere, Scott Widener and Shirley Wong.

Martin Krall and Mark Rotenstreich of *The News'* legal department were an important resource, as were Adrienne Rhodes in media relations and Yvette Reyes in John Campi's office. We also benefited greatly from the public-relations know-how of Sean Cassidy and Jeff Levinsohn at Dan Klores Associates.

Two men stand out for their generosity and professionalism as we assembled the elements of *Drawing a Crowd*. Harris Lewine passed along material from an earlier collaboration with Bill without hesitation and with only good will for our venture. He is a true gentleman.

ACKNOWLEDGMENTS

The authors will always be grateful to Pete Hamill for his personal commitment and masterly contribution to this book. We got to see in action the qualities that have earned him the admiration of many in journalism: the extraordinary writing, a belief in the mission of newspapers, a fundamental decency. To borrow a figure from elsewhere in these pages, dealing with Pete Hamill is like catch-ing a few innings of Koufax. The experience leaves you mightily impressed.

In the course of preparing this book, we were reminded of the many great pros who built *The News* into a champion tabloid and of the exceptional men who helped Bill along the way: among them, Pete Coutros, Dick Young, Jimmy Powers, Frank Graham, Gene McHugh, Bob Shand, Ed Sullivan, Worth Gatewood, Jim McCulley, Rube Goldberg and, of course, Bill's mentor, Leo O'Mealia.

Finally, no team can succeed without the backing of their home fans. Bill's wife, Dolores, was a source of inspiration and confidence, while Diane, Paige and Cameron Cornell were ever in Phil's thoughts and heart.

Bill Gallo and Phil Cornell
New York, New York

ABOUT BILL GALLO

by PETE HAMILL

I knew Bill Gallo before I ever met him. Every morning, usually in the jammed cars of a New York subway train, Gallo showed up, had something to say to me, made me smile, or think, or disagree, and then vanished.

He first made his entrance in the mid-1950s, slyly at first, in the pages of the New York *Daily News*. Captain Patterson's wonderful tabloid newspaper had been a part of my life since I was a boy in Brooklyn during World War II. My father and mother read it for news about the war, or about socialites who had run off with ironworkers, or murderers walking the last mile to what everyone called the hot seat. They were both immigrants from Northern Ireland, and that newspaper was their primary guide to the amazements of America, or more exactly, to that part of America called New York. My father devoured the sports section. My mother was entranced by Milton Caniff's beautifully sophisticated comic strip, "Terry and the Pirates." I reveled in "Dick Tracy" and its ghastly cast of victims. While I followed Tracy's pursuit of the terrible Flattop, or Shaky, or Shoulders, Bill Gallo was a combat Marine on Iwo Jima.

By 1946, when I was eleven, I wanted to be a cartoonist. The fundamental textbook for such an ambition was the *Daily News*, because it carried most of the greatest of the daily strips. "Tracy" and "Terry," but also "Moon Mullins" and "Little Orphan Annie" and "Smilin' Jack" and others now forgotten. In those days, they were not jammed into a comics ghetto, looking like a badly arranged amateur stamp album. They ran full-width across the top or bottom of a page, and were scattered through the run of the newspaper. The lettering in the balloons could be read. The subtlety of the drawing could be examined. The blacks were very black. It was the glory time of the newspaper cartoonist. And somewhere in the Art Deco masterpiece called The News Building, Bill Gallo, now a survivor of the Pacific war, was a copyboy, inspired by the same work, and acquiring the tools he would need to someday join the ranks of the *Daily News* masters.

By the mid-1950s, spot cartoons by Bill Gallo were appearing in the sports pages, which is where I first met him during my morning travels on the D train. Elsewhere in this book, he tells the story of that long apprenticeship. But I remember noticing his work during one hot summer while the Dodgers were still in Brooklyn. It must have been 1956. By then I was twenty-one years old and out of the Navy, and my own artistic ambitions had shifted. I wanted now to be a painter, and that fall I would travel to Mexico to attend art school on the G.I. Bill. But my love for cartooning was still a private passion; I admired Willard Mullin, Caniff, Roy Crane, Hal Foster, Burne Hogarth and a dozen others whose skills continued to amaze me. The sports cartoonist for the *Daily News* was Leo O'Mealia, but he had been meshed with the general consciousness of our Brooklyn flat for so long it would be inaccurate to say I admired him. He was one of the family, part of the dailiness of our lives. O'Mealia was a fine draftsman with a pen, his figures bursting with energy, his compositions simple and powerful, his drawings made up of hundreds of perfectly etched lines. Gallo's spots were different: bolder, blacker, executed with a brush. They caught my eye, because he was the kind of cartoonist I had dreamed of becoming.

By 1960, everything had changed. I had failed

out of painting into writing, and that summer began my newspaper career as a reporter for the *New York Post*. In the same year, Leo O'Mealia died, and Bill Gallo stepped in as his replacement. Every day, working for the *Post*, I read all the other newspapers. And it was clear that Gallo was becoming an essential part of the *Daily News*.

Bill Gallo showed his strengths almost from the beginning. He was, before everything else, a cartoonist who understood the absolute necessity of an idea. He wasn't doping imitation photographs, or simple caricatures; such work could be only a luxury on a tabloid newspaper. Gallo seemed to believe that it was wonderful to be a fine and elegant draftsman, but such refinements of style would not matter at all if the cartoon was not driven by an idea. His work was not there to be admired, like an opera singer's splendid voice; it was intended to be *felt*. Like all good tabloid journalism, Day after day, and eventually, decade after decade, Gallo found a way to express something fresh and original about his chosen subject: the world of sports. That world was already essential to the several million readers of the *Daily News*; many read their newspaper from back to front, that is, starting with the sports pages. In many ways, those sports pages were a major unifying force in New York, joining immigrant fathers closer to their American children, bringing together all races, all ethnic groups. They were not in the service of conflict. And Gallo, being the man he was, never fed the streams of meanness or incivility.

He had one additional, unstated mission. When Gallo became the lead cartoonist of the *Daily News*, there was a great hole in the heart of many New York sports fans: the departure at the end of 1957 of the Brooklyn Dodgers and the New York Giants to the golden pastures of the West Coast. For many fans, the essential attitude towards all baseball was one of deep, grieving bitterness. They had loved those teams—particularly the Dodgers—but they had been told by the greedy team owners that the relationship was all a big fraud. It was only about money. The Dodger and Giant fans vowed never to forget, never to forgive. Among the many casualties of that wounding experience were newspapers. After 1957, the *Daily News*, and other newspapers, began a long slow decline in circulation. This was usually—and glibly—blamed on the rise of television. But for sports fans, there was at least one other reason to stop reading the paper: the departure of those baseball teams. Divorce is never pleasant.

At the *Daily News*, Bill Gallo was one of the people who began to halt the decline. When the New York Mets started playing National League baseball in 1962, Gallo had already hit his stride. He found a way to embrace the inept Mets, to create a climate of affection and cordiality and welcome. The Mets were not the Dodgers. They were not the Giants. But what the hell: it was baseball and it was wonderful. In that sense, Gallo was an agent of healing.

In another important way, Gallo was able to assert some balance in the sports section. A kind of American innocence had ended on November 22, 1963, on a street outside the Texas Book Depository in Dallas. Something broke in many of us, even the most hardened New Yorkers. A belief in continuity. Or compromise. Or grace. As the disruptions of the 1960s gathered momentum, there were no longer any sacred cows in America. The Presidency itself was under relentless assault, its very legitimacy called into question by the worsening debacle of Vietnam. Bad manners became the norm. Everyone in the public arena was a suspect. Many reporters moved past skepticism into cynicism. The sports sections were not immune.

Gallo did not succumb to the general nastiness that was infecting the coverage of sports. He was not naive. And nobody who had fought at Iwo Jima could ever be indifferent to a distant war. But he maintained a clear attitude, which was to last until the present day: these are games. Some of them are brutal, but even boxing can be redeemed by the courage and skill of those who honor its codes. In his cartoons, in his weekly column, he made clear what he valued, without ever preaching a sermon.

Above all other qualities, Bill Gallo honored courage. That vague word that Ernest Hemingway once defined as "grace under pressure." He knew that you could never know about the greatness of a prizefighter until the fighter had been knocked down. The great ones always got up. That was true of other sports, too. You knew more about a man or woman in defeat than could ever be learned in victory. Great ballplayers went hitless for days, and did not give up; they took deep breaths and extra batting practice, reached for a bat and went again to the plate. Football players could be smashed into the tundra of a winter playing field; they came back in the next quarter. Winning and losing were part of the deal, but the best story was always in the loser's dressing room.

So, yes, Gallo implied in his work: these are games. But they are also metaphors for life. Only a tiny fraction of the young can ever become professional athletes. But all of us, even mere spectators, can learn from the rituals of the games. Gallo would never get fancy about any of this, but his attitudes have reflected such timeless notions almost from the beginning. One reason was rooted in his own character. Bill Gallo possesses that most valuable of all human attitudes: a sense of proportion. There are things much worse than the loss of a sporting contest. The death of a child. The loss of a loved one. War.

He also has demonstrated that a man can work for a lifetime at the craft of journalism without being hardened by its numbing repetitive examples of human folly. Some newspapermen become like old cops; they have seen so much human lousiness they have no time for the rest of the human race. Not Gallo. I got to know him in the early 1960s, meeting him at a Floyd Patterson fight camp in the Catskills. That summer I was pulled off the city desk to sub for the *Post's* boxing writer, Al Buck, while he was on vacation. I was just another byline, happy in my work, but certainly nobody worth remembering. That day, Bill Gallo treated me as if I were one of the stars of sports journalism. Jimmy Cannon or Red Smith. Jesse Abramson or Leonard Shecter. Sure, I worked for a competing newspaper. That didn't matter to Gallo. We were members of the same rude guild. He introduced me to the trainers, the sparring partners, the other beat reporters. He showed me where to get a cup of coffee. He made certain I was fed. In short, he was a gentleman. His manners have always been impeccable, but on that day, long ago, he was showing another characteristic that is rarer than it should be in all professions: he was (and is) kind to the tentative and uniformed young.

In all the years since, those qualities have never changed. Across those decades, we have seen each other at boxing shows. We've sometimes found ourselves together in a press box at a ballpark or at sports dinners or at events staged by the National Cartoonists Society. I worked with him for three years at the *Daily News* in the 1970s; in 1997, I was editor-in-chief of that newspaper, and he was always a source of common sense, institutional memory and grace. He didn't work for me; we both worked for the *Daily News*. We shared a common goal: to make the newspaper better. On days of aggravation and distraction, I liked to wander down to the room where he made his cartoons, and talk about the paper, and great cartoonists, and old fighters. He hated the exhausting silliness of office politics. He wished that more people in the newspaper business loved it as much as we did. I remember thinking, not for the first time, that if I ever were pinned down in a foxhole, I'd want Bill Gallo beside me.

Today, Bill continues to draw cartoons for that newspaper, providing it with a tone and a visual identity that simply can't be duplicated. Bill Gallo is Bill Gallo and nobody can be another Bill Gallo anymore than a young fighter can be another Sugar Ray Robinson. But there is something stark about his position at the turn of the century: Gallo is one of the last sports cartoonists in the United States, the country that invented the form. We live in an era of great editorial cartoonists, but there is no upcoming generation of cartoonists who focus their talents on sports. Few contemporary editors, and almost no publishers, understand how important sports cartoons can be to their newspapers. It's easier, and cheaper, to paste still another AP photo into the sports pages. And because there are so few sports cartoonists, the gifted young don't dream of being Willard Mullin or Tad Dorgan or

Bill Gallo. That loss of a certain kind of youthful desire impoverishes those newspapers. But it also makes this a poorer country. All great cartoonists try to express a big simple truth that lurks elusively beneath the stacking of facts. These days, they do it only for politics, and almost never for sports, the true national obsession.

I hope this book is read by many sports fans and the countless fans of Bill Gallo. But it would serve a larger purpose if it were read by newspaper publishers, who determine budgets, and editors, who decide about content. They might see their way to hire the next Bill Gallo. Not an imitator. But some-

one who understands the power of the idea and the place of sports in the mind of the city. If they do, this book will be an inspiration and a guide to that young unknown cartoonist who is hunched over a drawing table tonight, trying to make sense of the facts through the use of talent. To follow the example of Bill Gallo, however, that youngster will also need qualities that go far beyond talent: grace, humor and an invincible sense of proportion. Such qualities are not taught in any school. But they are here, in the pages of this book.

GATHERING A CROWD

by PHIL CORNELL

By his own estimate, Bill Gallo has contributed 14,000 sports cartoons to the *Daily News* over the past four decades. And yet, the inspiration for *Drawing a Crowd* was not one of Bill's illustrations but his words, specifically a column that ran in *The News* on August 10, 1997, under the headline: "It Doesn't Get Much Better Than This."

"In this imperfect world," wrote Gallo, "there are times when you look at something and say, 'Yes, this is perfection.'" He offered a lifetime's worth of examples, from his wife's paella to the Ali punch that dropped big bad George Foreman in

Zaire, from the grace of DiMaggio to the utilitarian splendor of the author's shoes.

It was an impressive rundown of people and events, made personal by the warmly appreciative voice of the narrator. I would eventually come to see this column as a kind of drawing too, a landscape formed with words instead of India ink. But at the time, I was simply overwhelmed by the sweep of this man's career. Suddenly, that stirring reminiscence itself seemed perfect as a springboard to a book-length retrospective.

Talking to Bill, I learned that such a project had

been proposed in the past—even attempted—but never realized. Not missing a beat, Gallo posed this challenge: line up a publisher and he would supply decades' worth of material. "We'll be partners," he shouted over his shoulder as he headed off. And even though the artist was sketching Mantle and Maris about the time I was learning to ride a two-wheeler, he truly meant equal partners. We continually consulted one another on just about everything that has gone into *Drawing a Crowd*.

One problem we immediately faced was the book's structure. How do you organize such a mass of time-rooted material? I quickly concluded that a parade of portraits or a rigid chronology would become drudgery for the reader. I didn't want to squander the element of surprise that keeps people turning the pages of a newspaper. So I suggested chapters based on themes, a structure that better suits Bill's emphasis on ideas and cross-references. My hope is that *Drawing a Crowd* can re-create the flavor of this artist's native habitat, the daily newspaper, since that is where virtually all these drawings were first seen.

Some of the text has previously appeared in *The News* too, including Gallo's reflections on Iwo Jima and Vietnam; observations about Koufax, Stengel and DiMaggio; his confession to being a Cardinals fan; the recognition of his predecessors in the field; and the aforementioned ponderings on perfection. Most of the text was generated specifically for this book, however, and to prime the pump of memory, I asked Bill every question I could think of about events in his life and career.

It was also important that we set a tone that can best be described as Two Guys Talkin' Sports, a Gallo calling card. This book couldn't be Two In-siders Talkin' Sports or Two Guys Who Do Nothing But Talk Sports. For much of the beauty of Bill Gallo is that he casts his net wide for ideas and wouldn't think of reducing life to a heap of sports stats.

During the preparation of this book, I learned a thing or two about how Bill goes about his work. I observed as he brushed in black ink to build drama within a cartoon panel, as if he were a cinematog-rapher in film noir. I noticed how he modulated the characters' voices by varying the thickness of his lettering. I marveled at his way of leaving some things unsaid or unseen or how he wisely turns to authors and philosophers to help articulate his mes-sage. I realized that his bold brush strokes are sub-stantial enough for an outlook that is at once humorous and sentimental and learned and fully engaged with life.

Just how engaged was apparent in a cartoon of Bill's that ran in *The News* as this book neared completion. At the top of the drawing, two kids in pajamas have exciting news to share with their mom: Dad said they could stay up late into the night to watch both the Yankees' and the Mets' play-off games on television. In the bottom half of the drawing, Dad is intently following the action—with the children fast asleep in his lap. While comment-ing on baseball's disregard for the young fan, Gallo tucks this observation into the corner: "Here's a wealthy man. He's got his kids—they're nice and quiet—and he's got a pocketful of subway tokens."

That kind of reality cuts through all the flash and noise and money surrounding sports and gets to what is truly important. Perhaps that's why Bill Gallo has spoken to millions of readers across many years and thousands of illustrations. He does so once more in *Drawing a Crowd*, even as he re-minds us of the glory and drama and humor in ath-letics. That he can do so each day within the confines of a single cartoon, well, it doesn't get much better than that.

FILLING IN
THE BACKGROUND

by BILL GALLO

I was attending a wake in the Irish Bronx many years ago when I ran into a guy I hadn't seen in a long, long time. He invited me to a nearby bar to catch up on our lives. "Funny thing about this bar," he added, "there's a cartoon of yours right over the cash register on the wall. A drawing of Jim Brown."

"It's not an original," I said.

"Yeah, I think it is," he countered. "Come on over."

My companion and I got to the bar and, sure enough, hanging on the wall was a cartoon of Jim Brown, one I had drawn during the great running back's playing days. A nice cartoon, framed and bearing my signature, but not personalized with a "To so-and-so."

"Where'd you get that?" I innocently asked the bartender.

"Oh that?" replied the burly barkeep. "That's Gallo. Gallo of *The News*. Do you know Gallo of *The News*? He gave it to me. He comes here all the time."

I was intrigued because I had never before set foot in the place. "You say he comes in here?"

"Yeah, all the time with friends, newspaper guys," the bartender responded.

My companion lowered the boom: "You know who you're talking to? You're talking to Bill Gallo of the *Daily News*. This is Bill Gallo."

I pressed my advantage over the suddenly flustered barman. "Now can you tell me where you got it?"

"I don't know. Somebody brought it in. I think he was a printer."

"From the *Daily News*?"

"Yeah, I think he was. I don't see him around anymore. I didn't have anything to do with it."

That's what four decades of illustrations in *The News* can do for a cartoonist. My creations—such as Basement Bertha, Yuchie, General Von Steingrabber and a pantheon of athletes—have fanned out into countless corners of Gotham and, judging from the mail I receive, into the everyday lives of working people. I have tried to reach these readers with humor and understanding, sentiment and fairness. No cheap shots, no condescension, no gloating.

I'm a big believer in connecting with the reader. I think of the reader as a whole, as one person, and I am that reader. Part of that reader is me. I know through years of talking sports with people that they share these sentiments. People know me; they know me by reading me, just like they know Jimmy Breslin or Pete Hamill or any other columnist. They know who they are. If you take a stand, they know you.

I've drawn many fabulously gifted sports figures, yet I relate my own life to the athlete who succeeds more on grit and determination than on natural talent. I'm like Eddie Stanky, the second baseman of the 1940s and early '50s. He was limited in skills, but he tried so hard it was said that "Eddie Stanky can't hit, can't throw, can't run, can't catch. The only thing he can do is beat you."

I admire those guys, the underdogs. I think most people feel the same way. They're not great, but they can be great if they work hard. I put myself in there. I never give up, and if I want something I'll scratch and claw and I'll get it. I'm Eddie Stanky (well, maybe not the part that got him nicknamed "the Brat"). There are better artists than me. There are better newspapermen than me. But put all the elements together, and I'll give you a run.

Above all, I have tried to say something to the reader every day through my illustrations. Deliver a theme, much like a columnist does. Early on, a journalist imparted to me sound advice: "It's not just drawing. Try to be a reporter first." I've heeded those words through many years and thousands of cartoons.

I give aspiring illustrators a similar message. After reminding them about the dwindling number of opportunities these days for sports cartoonists, I tell them to first get a newspaper job, any job, just be around a newspaper to see how it works. All the while, keep up your drawing and do some writing, too. Offer pieces of interest to the editors.

GROWING UP

From as young as seven, I had my sights set on working for a newspaper. Like countless generations have learned any occupation, I became entranced watching my father do it. Francisco "Frank" Gallo was a reporter and editor for *La Prensa*, a newspaper that served 25,000 transplanted Spaniards in New York. My father fit this demographic himself. He had traveled from the seaport of Santander, near northern Spain's Basque country, to New York by way of Cuba, arriving here in 1919. Meanwhile, an aspiring concert pianist, Henrietta Cabellero, had made a similar odyssey from Barcelona to Buenos Aires to the Big Apple. They met in an English class, and the next generation of Gallos was assured.

I was the middle of three children, between an older sister, Gloria (now deceased), and a younger brother, Henry. I spent the first year of my life in Harlem, then my family migrated across the 59th Street Bridge to the more open spaces of Astoria, Queens.

As a kid, I always drew. Pencils, crayons, whatever I had. I was encouraged by my mother to keep it up. I also frequented the sandlots of Astoria to play baseball, gobbling up grounders at second base and indulging the long-rumored fantasy that a major-league scout might be in attendance. (Scouts did turn out for a neighborhood boy named Eddie Ford, later known as Whitey.)

My father covered a lot of sporting events for his paper, and he often took me along. He was especially interested in boxing—he once was part-manager of a Cuban welterweight—and that was how I began watching prizefights. The sight of two men trying to slug each other into unconsciousness is not normally considered children's entertainment, but I was enthralled. To this day, I have a special respect and affinity for that sport.

I loved to go to Papa's paper as well. I relished the smell of the ink and felt terrific in that atmosphere. All the while growing up, I used to think that a great way to make a living was to be a writer for a newspaper. Then I looked at some of the sports cartoonists, like Burris Jenkins, Jr., in the *Journal-American*, and the *World-Telegram*'s Willard Mullin, creator of the Brooklyn Dodgers "Bum," and I thought, "Boy, this is even better than writing. You get to tell your story by drawing a picture, and you can tell it better even." Every paper had a sports cartoonist back then, and I used to marvel at them. Along with the sports columnist, the cartoonist was the star of the paper. I kind of liked that.

The apprenticeship with my father was cut painfully short, for he died in 1934 at age thirty-six, when I was just eleven. The suddenness of his death stays with me still. He contracted walking pneumonia and became so sick he was taken to the hospital, never to return. A man who was as healthy as a bear all his life was gone within a week of getting sick. Antibiotics were unknown then; if they'd had penicillin at the time, my father would have made it.

With our breadwinner gone, our family's standard of living suffered. We had to move to a poorer neighborhood, and that was the beginning of my growing up. I took a variety of Depression-era jobs, from working at a grocery for bundles of food to scavenging for lumps of coal in the Long Island City train yards. I also served as a messenger out of Saks Fifth Avenue's cellar and sold supplies to drugstores. In the meantime, I commuted to Manhattan's Benjamin Franklin High School because it offered art classes where I could pursue my drawing.

JOINING *THE NEWS*

After graduation in 1941, I applied for a copyboy's job at every newspaper in New York—and there were lots of them back then. I had opportunities to work for the *Mirror* or *The News*. I had to choose. As I got off the train that day, it was raining and *The News* was closer. So I picked *The News*.

My career at the *Daily News* began on October 8, 1941, in the entry-level job of copyboy or "picture clerk." You'd sit on the copy bench and wait to assist a reporter or editor, doing everything from writing captions to fetching coffee, absorbing knowledge from some of the best pros in the business. That was our reporting school, and many a crusty old newspaper guy would tell you that one year chasing "copy" was better than four years of journalism in college.

During World War II, though, Uncle Sam outranked any editor, and on December 8, 1942, two weeks before my twentieth birthday, I joined the Marines. Every able-bodied male was answering the call back then, and I figured the Marines, with their superior training, would give me the best chance of survival. That belief was shaken mightily when I got to Parris Island and the drill instructor addressed the new recruits. "Eighty percent of you guys are going to be dead in six months," he informed us. "So I'm talking to the twenty percent who are going to make it. It's up to you who's going to make that twenty percent." I thought, "There's not much of a future here."

It turned out that I did have a future, though, as a demolitions technician, even if dengue landed

THE ART OF SPORTS CARTOONING

WILLARD MULLIN 1902–1978.

ASIDE TO ASPIRING SPORTS CARTOONISTS: GENTLEMEN, THIS WAS THE MAN. NOBODY DID IT BETTER! —BUSCEMA

me in the hospital and the percussion cap of a Japanese hand grenade I was dismantling went off in my hand. I saw combat in four major battles in the Pacific Theater, including Iwo Jima, all the while concentrating on one thing: survival, to be in the twenty percent who make it back.

After the war, I returned to *The News*, became an apprentice in the art department and added to my formal education. I studied at the Cartoonists and Illustrators School—later the School of Visual Arts—and attended Columbia University under the new G.I. Bill as a liberal arts major.

By then, I had developed another passion besides newspapers: Dolores Rodriguez. My mother had known her mother, and because she was a model, I could admire her in a Lord & Taylor ad in *The New York Times*. Our romance blossomed after the war, and we were married in 1950.

As we started a family, school became a luxury. To make more money, I moonlighted at the *Brooklyn Eagle*, laying out pages and writing captions. I was doing similar work at *The News*, plus covering stories on my own and taking on any other task that would make me a more complete newspaperman. Typically, my initiative didn't mean any extra money. I did it because I wanted to get better, and I wanted the paper to be better. That was reward enough.

During this period, I was gravitating toward sports. I drew the small illustrations once used to break up text in sports columns, and in April 1954 broke through with a full-blown boxing illustration titled "Hitting Spree," which recounted a match between a pair of long-forgotten middleweights, George Johnson and Moses Ward. Later that year, I supplied a similar recap of a welterweight championship bout between Kid Gavilan and Johnny Saxton.

In the 1950s, *The News* had a star cartoonist of its own, Leo O'Mealia, a veteran of comic strips and comic book adventures who created one of the paper's more famous front pages. Leo the Lion, as he was known, had immortalized the Brooklyn Dodgers' 1955 victory over their World Series nemesis, the New York Yankees, by drawing an open-mouthed, wide-eyed hobo. The headline proclaimed, "Who's a Bum!" The drawing board he used for that memorable image, as well as a picture of the artist himself, hold a prominent spot on my office wall to this day.

Hitting Spree

By Bill Gallo

YOU'RE GOING WITH ME!

WARD ALMOST WRESTLED JOHNSON TO THE CANVAS AFTER BEING FLOORED IN 4TH.

MOSES WAS LEADING TILL THE FOURTH WHEN JOHNSON CAUGHT HIM IN HIS OWN CORNER AND PITCHED LEFTS AND RIGHTS FOR ALMOST A FULL MINUTE.

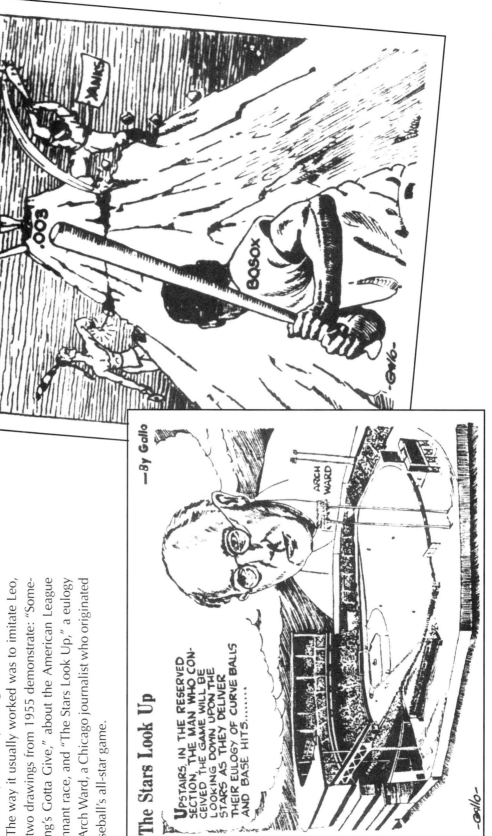

Something's Gotta Give —By Gallo

The Stars Look Up —By Gallo

UPSTAIRS, IN THE RESERVED
SECTION, THE MAN WHO CON-
CEIVED THE GAME WILL BE
LOOKING DOWN UPON THE
STARS AS THEY DELIVER
THEIR EULOGY OF CURVE BALLS
AND BASE HITS........

Leo was my mentor at *The News,* and he stressed an important lesson to me: sacrifice the drawing for the idea. It was a principle that had been imparted to him by Thomas Aloysius Dorgan, also known as TAD, the renowned cartoonist of the *New York Evening Journal.*

Leo was an invaluable source of encouragement when I faced frustration. "Work the drawing one way," he advised, "and if that doesn't work, try it another way. But keep doing it."

The way it usually worked was to imitate Leo, as two drawings from 1955 demonstrate: "Something's Gotta Give," about the American League pennant race, and "The Stars Look Up," a eulogy to Arch Ward, a Chicago journalist who originated baseball's all-star game.

FILLING IN THE BACKGROUND

Even after Leo's death in 1960, when I succeeded him as sports cartoonist, the expectation of managing editor Robert Shand was that I would simply perpetuate O'Mealia's style, be sort of a Leo Part II. I did just that at first, because I wanted the job, but I didn't feel good about it.

Leo was a terrific draftsman, an excellent pen-and-ink man—line by line, never used a brush—and he had an awful lot of patience. I liked a looser, more spontaneous style, and I didn't want to get tied down to the art. So every once in a while, I'd veer into my own thing. Shand didn't like it, though. I got fed up and told my wife, "It was a nice promotion, but I'm going to quit it. I'll probably be asked to be a reporter on cityside or go back to retouching in the art department. Anything." She backed me all the way.

One day, after Shand had bawled me out about something I had done on my own, I went to him and said, "Thanks for the opportunity, but I quit this particular job."

"Why?" he inquired.

"I can't do Leo O'Mealia, because I don't want to," I told him. "I have my own ideas. I have my own way of doing things."

I figured it was all over for me as a sports cartoonist. But first I had to do one more illustration, a boxing drawing, that would be my last. I was working on it, "The Way We Saw It," when Shand showed up at my desk.

"From now on, you do it your way," he said. I was forever grateful to him. That was the turning point. For the first time I felt the job was mine. Free of those restrictions, I developed my own style and outlook, stationed at ringside, on the football sidelines or in a World Series press box. I've always tried to make it easy on the reader, whether I'm writing or drawing. Make it simple and natural on his eyes so he doesn't have to strain and wonder, "Who is this? What is that?" After all, the reader is going to own that paper for only a half-hour of his life. He'll quit on you if you make him struggle.

I don't expect to please everybody with my drawings, and why would anyone want to? The people who fight you and your ideas are just as valuable as the people who praise you. You're doing something for them. You're helping them form some kind of opinion, for or against.

Still, the majority of the readers do like me, and that's what keeps me going. As long as the plus side of the ledger is ahead of the negative side, you're doing all right.

The Way We Saw It —By Gallo

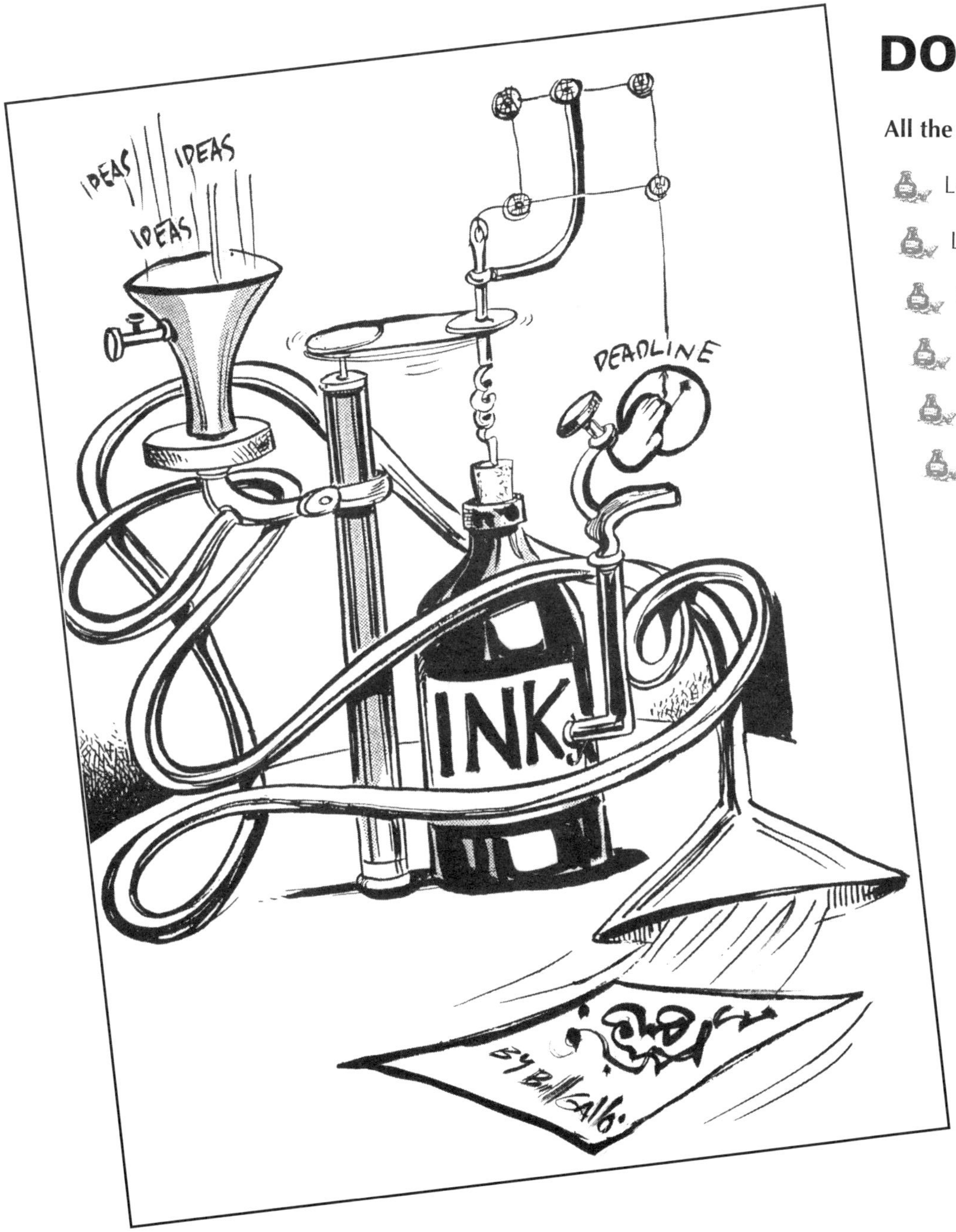

DOING A CARTOON IS EASY

All the cartoonist has to do is . . .

Load up the funnel with ideas

Let them pass through the thinking process

Hold back the deadline clock

Let the thoughts spin around in the India ink

Allow the ink to dry as it passes through the tube

And watch as out comes the finished product.

FILLING IN THE BACKGROUND

LISTENING TO THE PUBLIC

Each day, I keep an ear out for what the average man or woman is talking about, and that gives me ideas for drawings. The thought is what comes first, sometimes many thoughts. Then I'll try it out in pencil. See how it looks. Sometimes it doesn't work out. What you see in your mind is clearer than the way you can put it on paper. So, I'll ditch that idea and try another way.

I'm thinking not only about how the subject looks, but the attitude, how he walks, his mannerisms. When you're a cartoonist, you look at people a little closer. You note the slope in Joe Namath's shoulders or the herky-jerky head tic that Mike Tyson had at the top of his game. You study the people's habits, and you don't leave anything out. I also go through the feeling of throwing a pass or a punch.

Usually, the first idea that hits me is the one I use, but there are times when I think, "I've done this before" or "I can do better than that." Then it's literally back to the drawing board.

Over the years, if I'd see anything that was interesting or might make a good picture with a caption, I'd send it in to the editors, and most would get in the paper. In a pinch, I could draw something in a

FROM START . . .

YOGI AND PARTNER - A RETURN TO THE BRIGHT LIGHTS

DRAWING A CROWD

half-hour, twenty minutes, with a ballpoint pen. A more intricate collage of several drawings might take a few hours or more at my desk, started in pencil and completed with ink. For a magazine, I give it a more finished appearance, drawn more carefully, but I enjoy the spontaneity of a daily newspaper. It's the essence of the business.

I approach my job these days with the same en-thusiasm that I had forty years ago. I still worry about deadlines. People tend to make a lot about age, but I don't think of myself as an old guy, never do. I go at it as a jolly, optimistic philosopher who looks skyward and says, "Don't bother me yet. I'm busy."

In any event, the family trade has been passed on to my son Greg, who is sports editor for the competition, the *New York Post*. My other son, Bill Jr., also has a track record in the sports world: a lifelong lover of horses, he is director of racing at the National Steeplechase in Maryland. My nephew Hank Gallo—before he went into television—was a feature writer and movie critic for *The News*. At least one of my four granddaughters, Amy, is going to college with ambitions to be a writer.

...TO FINISH

FILLING IN THE BACKGROUND

A PROUD TRADITION

It's a great thing to be a sports cartoonist, a noble profession that I trace back at least to Goya's paintings of bullfights. More recently, there was the humor and intelligence of TAD, who had a following like no other sports cartoonist before or since. The man who coined such beloved bits of the vernacular as "hot dog," "the cat's meow" and "for crying out loud" died in 1929 but produced such quality work that the *Journal-American* reprinted it into the 1940s.

There were great ones like Rube Goldberg, Bob Edgren, Robert Ripley (of subsequent "Believe It or Not" fame), Hype Igoe and Bud Fisher. Later came Burris Jenkins, Jr., Bill Crawford, Tom Paprocki, O'Mealia and Willard Mullin, the greatest of them all. "What did Mullin have today?" was heard daily during his time.

Bruce Stark worked at *The News* with me, and his artistry is still revered; today you see a similar level of skill in the caricatures of Ed Murawinski. Len Hollrieser was a good one, and so were Murray Olderman, Lou Darvas, Bob Coyne, Alan Maver, Bil Canfield, and Charlie McGill. There aren't many of us left now, since papers have gotten out of the habit of hiring sports cartoonists, which discouraged a lot of kids who could draw. That makes me a dinosaur of sorts, a bison.

I've been at it a good long while now,

and I always get a kick out of answering the No. 1 question people put to me: "How long does it take you to draw a cartoon?" My short answer is, "About two hours and forty years."

The longer answer will unfold, I hope, in the pages of this book. This is sports as I've seen it through the years, from my drawing board. It's there that I find I can tell a story best. Read on!

SPORTS CARTOONIST LESSON—NO. 1

① FIRST YOU DRAW A GOOD EGG...

② ...THEN YOU PUT IN YOUR GUIDE LINES...
CAP LINE
NOSE →
← EYES
← MOUTH

③ DRAW IN THE EARS USING EYE AND NOSE LINES FOR TOP AND BOTTOM...

④ ...BEGIN FOCUSING IN ON LIKENESS

⑤ ...WORK ON DISTINGUISHING FEATURES...

⑥ ...AND, VOILA'! (MAKE SURE, WHEN NOT IDENTIFYING, THE FACE IS...

CHAPTER ONE

THE RING OF TRUTH

WINNER BY A KNOCKOUT

I grew up around boxing, which may explain why I like the sport, particularly the combat of it. I boxed in the Marine Corps, but never in anger. If an opponent became so enraged that he'd say, "Take the gloves off," he wasn't the guy I'd want to box. We're playing a game here, man.

Boxers themselves are a noble bunch. Some of them don't realize they're noble, but it's such a basic thing, one man against another. It almost sounds brutal and inhuman, yet it's a great contest when done right. And sometimes you can call it art. You've got to be pretty secure to walk those four steps into the ring. It's more than the other man you're facing—it's the fear of failure. And you face that alone.

Of course, some boxers do it too long, and that's when it gets sad. That's why I always fight for a pension fund. Also, some of them are not the best of citizens. Generally speaking, though, they are a noble bunch. Even Mike Tyson, there's a nobility about him when he enters the ring.

I drew this illustration of Tyson when he started to attract attention in the mid-'80s, emphasizing his strength and power in a single punch. He's small for a heavyweight, 5-foot-10 or -11, and he was knocking out big guys, bowling them over. He had quick choppy steps, and he pranced around the ring, waiting for the fight to begin. You could almost feel his impatience for that bell.

PERFECTION IN PUGILISM

As far as I'm concerned, Sugar Ray Robinson was the greatest boxer of them all. In fact, among newspapermen watching him, it was almost unanimous that he was the greatest. That was a very easy call. It was like somebody watching Fred Astaire in action and saying, "Can he dance?"

Once the bell rang, he became a craftsman, an artist and a killer all in one. Before the bell, he was calm and relaxed, almost like he could take a nap on his stool. I tried to convey that ease—and the dream he represented to young fighters—with a Golden Gloves drawing.

My portrait for his April 1989 obituary recalled the Sugar Ray of a half-century before, when he was an amateur and his hair flew around during a fight. That was the beginning, 1939. What follows is the end, his retirement from the ring in 1965:

"Ladies and gentlemen," the Garden loudspeakers announced, "the greatest fighter who ever lived, Sugar Ray Robinson."

The fans were up on their feet, banging their hands together and cheering. Up the middle aisle from the 50th Street side [of the old Madison Square Garden], he came. He climbed into the ring, walked gracefully to the center, held his arms outstretched, smiled humbly, shook his head. He bowed from the waist, very Oriental, turned and bowed from the waist to the other side. You expected him to say, "Sayonara." Instead, before it was over, he said, "A tout à l'heure."

"In English," said Sugar Ray, "that means, 'I'll see you later.'"

—from my *Daily News* account of Sugar Ray Robinson's farewell to boxing, December 11, 1965

1940
SUGAR RAY ROBINSON, 135-POUND OPEN **GOLDEN GLOVES** CHAMPION. WENT ON TO BECOME THE GREATEST FIGHTER OF OUR TIME— THE **PICASSO** OF THE RING.

TONIGHT, ALONE FOR A SPLIT SECOND, A KID DREAMS — DREAMS OF PICASSO.

HOW SWEET IT WAS

THE INCOMPARABLE SUGAR RAY ROBINSON (WALKER SMITH, JR.) 1939—126 POUND **GOLDEN GLOVES** OPEN CHAMPION

THE BEGINNING

MIDDLEWEIGHT CHAMP (1951 TO 1954) MIDDLEWEIGHT CHAMP (1955 TO 1960)

THE PROS:
TOTAL BOUTS—200
WINS—175
KO'S—110
WELTERWEIGHT CHAMP (1946 TO 1951)

MMTER, WE WILL NOT SEE THE LIKES OF HIM AGAIN. THAT KIND OF BOXING TALENT COMES AROUND EVERY 100 YEARS!

Pages 75-77

KING OF THE RING: Former middleweight boxing champion Sugar Ray Robinson, who died yesterday at the age of 67, is remembered by Mike Lupica, Michael Katz and Vic Ziegel.

DEMPSEY THE LIONHEARTED

One of Jack Dempsey's more famous fights was against Luis Firpo in 1923. That was the bout in which Firpo knocked Dempsey out of the ring, but Jack came back to stop him in the second round. My father loved Jack Dempsey, but blood is thicker than water, and he bet on Firpo, the Argentine. Years later, when I met Dempsey as an adult, I told him about that and he got a big kick out of it.

These drawings are from when Jack sat for me in 1980, three years before he died. Sometimes, even when he was looking mean, like a lion, he was actually very happy. That's the case in the cartoon to the right. There was a lot of character in his face, a lot of the Indian in him. He was a solid, stoic guy—sphinx-like and very strong—yet a gentle soul. From that session, I remember he had paintings by George Bellows on his apartment walls (though not the famous one of Firpo punching Dempsey through the ropes).

Dempsey once told me he believed in reincarnation. His wife got him interested. I took it as a gag, but then he got serious. So I said, "Jack, what would you want to come back as?" He said, "Well, I wouldn't want to be the heavyweight champ or anything like that. I've had that. I'd like to come back as a lion."

"THE CHAMP" BY BILL GALLO. SKETCHED AT JACK DEMPSEY'S N.Y. APT.— HE WAS IN HIS 80's AT THE TIME

"I was always grateful to the town, the way they treated me."

"at 80 I discovered opera and I like it."

"Barne is my sweetheart. It's the absolute best number one."

Bill Gallo.

A VISIT FROM JOE LOUIS

In April 1976, I was hunched over my drawing board, finishing a cartoon about the Mets, when I sensed someone looking over my shoulder. I looked up and there was Joe Louis, the greatest heavyweight I had ever seen, looming over me.

"How're you doing?" he asked in his easy way. Joe had been in the sports department that day as a guest of Jim McCulley, then the paper's boxing writer. I asked Joe to sit at the next desk and pose for a sketch. He did, and when it was finished, I asked him to autograph it. The champ took the India-ink pen I used and signed it at the bottom of the drawing.

Whenever I hear that tired old phrase "White Hope," I have to smile and think of Joe Louis. When Louis was champion, all the white guys I knew rooted for him, and he fought mainly white fighters. This was a tribute to the man, for he was boxing in those days.

Joe never bragged, though; he was such a modest, noble man. A brash, young Muhammad Ali once said to Louis: "All you did was fight the Bum of the Month." Joe just replied, "You know, you would have been on that list."

Louis was famous his entire adult life and yet gave fame little importance. Once, when he was a greeter at Caesars Palace, a young woman asked him, "Can I have your autograph, Mr. Newcombe?" mistaking him for former Dodger pitcher Don Newcombe. Joe, not wanting to embarrass the lady, took pad and pen in hand and whispered to an onlooker, "How do you spell Newcombe?"

...AND WE GOT THE CHAMP TO AUTOGRAPH IT FOR US.

DEAR BOSS — SORRY I WON'T HAVE TIME TO DO A CARTOON TODAY. I HAD TO ESCORT AN OLD FRIEND AROUND THE NEWS' BUILDING. — B.G.

THE RING OF TRUTH

A MATCH MADE IN HEAVEN

Rivalries like Pep-Saddler, Dempsey-Tunney or Ali-Frazier were beauts, all unforgettable, but Tony Zale-Rocky Graziano goes to the head of the charts. Rocky Graziano, a dead-end kid from New York, vs. Tony Zale, a serious tough guy from Gary, Indiana, where steel is refined.

Fights? More like wars. Two middleweight champs going toe to toe from the opening bell, trying to kill one another. Zale goes down, then Rocky hits the canvas, then Zale again, then Graziano smells the resin. These two great battlers gave returning World War II veterans three terrific shows in the late '40s, Zale winning two of them.

I drew this in 1997, when Tony died. As tough and as hard as he was inside the ropes, Zale was a mild-mannered gentleman outside of them. "I developed a terrible shyness," he explained. "I couldn't face people. . . . In boxing, it was always a different story for me. I had just one man to reckon with."

They're both gone now—Graziano died in 1990—but I like to think they're smiling down on us, recalling the glorious time when they were kings of the ring. What could Rocky be saying? "Tony, somebody up here likes us."

IN THE HUNT WITH MARCIANO

Rocky Marciano, the only undefeated heavyweight champ, was so intense, so dogged, so never-give-up. Marciano claims he never was scared—in the ring—and you had to believe him.

Rocky stalked his opponent during a fight, like he was going after his prey. That's what I was after in the 1989 illustration at left, drawn twenty years after his death in

a plane crash: that feeling of "Here I come, coming after you." You knew Marciano was going to get his man. You knew it because *he* knew it. Even in his 1952 fight with Jersey Joe Walcott, when he was so far behind, you always sensed he was going to get him—and he did, in the thirteenth round, with a cruncher of a punch, which I recalled in a magazine illustration many years later.

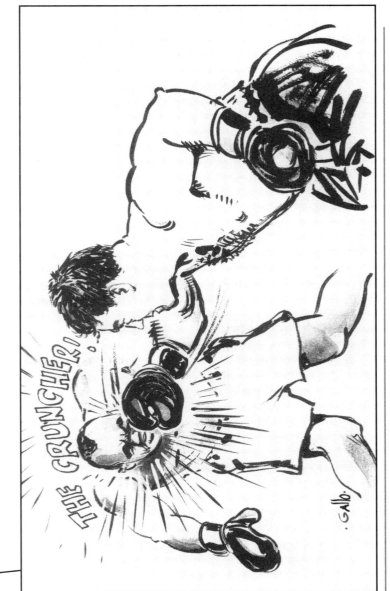

THE CRUNCHER!

ROCKY MARCIANO
(THE BROCKTON BLOCKBUSTER)
TOTAL BOUTS - 49
KO'S - 43
W.D - 6
• HEAVYWEIGHT CHAMPION - 1952 to 1956
• HALL OF FAME - 1959

SONNY YET OVERCAST

I was once asked if Sonny Liston was the Tyson of his day. I replied no, no. I always got along with Tyson in the beginning. Liston was a surly guy. He seemed angry at the press. He was a helluva fighter, but he was not cooperative. He seemed to be on the defensive all the time and was a very hard man to interview. He would kind of ignore you, look at you and give you a "yes" or a "no." He would listen to jazz while he trained, playing it loud as he skipped rope.

When he fought Ali the first time, in 1964, you had to flip a coin to see who you disliked more, because Ali wasn't popular then either. I didn't like Liston at all, but, of course, I got to like Ali.

This drawing recalled Liston's infamous one-round loss to Ali in their 1965 rematch and was done on the occasion of his death at the end of 1970.

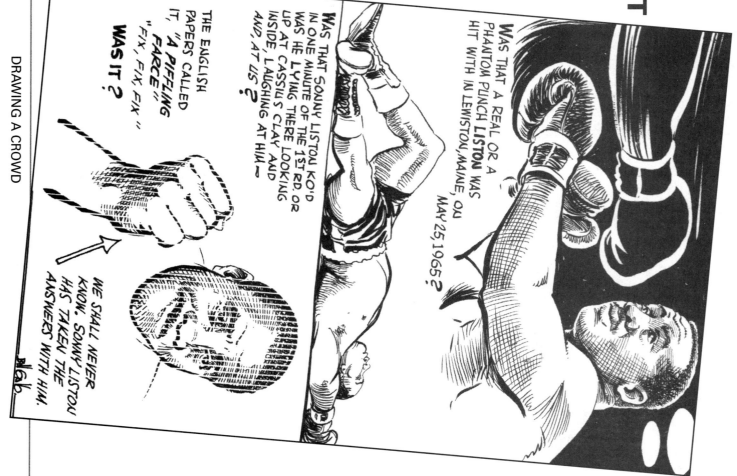

HE HAD IT SEWN UP

Ray Mancini's father was a lightweight fighter, the original Boom-Boom. He had to go off to war and so had to give up his dream of becoming lightweight champion. Ray wanted to do for his father what his father couldn't do for himself—and he did, by winning that title in 1982.

Ray was a nice kid who took too many punches; even when he won, he got cut up. This cartoon from February 1985 dramatized the toll boxing was taking on Mancini. I invoked the words of an authority on absorbing punishment in the ring: heavyweight Chuck Wepner, "The Bayonne Bleeder," who once fought Ali. I used to say that Wepner was so prone to cuts, he started bleeding at the prefight handshake.

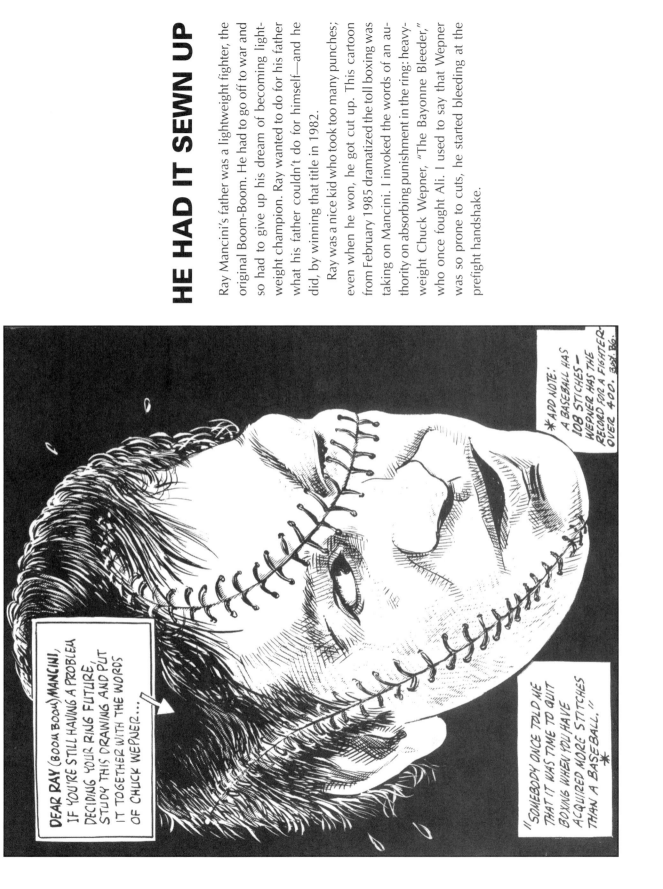

A BEATEN MAN

I always had a sketch pad with me at ringside. It came in handy when I saw this four-round fighter take a shellacking. His handler wouldn't stop the mismatch, so the referee said, "Look, you've had enough, kid." I made a quick sketch of that, and then I made a painting. I later used it as a cartoon. I'd date it about 1975.

The perspective is intended to lead your eye up the boxer's body, to his head and bloody cuts. You see the compassion of the ref without even seeing his face, just by the way he's holding him, like a father would a son.

You can't possibly argue that boxing isn't brutal. Brutal it is. One man is trying to knock out another man with his fist, which is essentially a club. But sometimes it gets into the category of art, and that's when you marvel at it. You marvel at the moves of a Willie Pep, great boxer that he was, and Sugar Ray Robinson and Muhammad Ali. You marvel at how the great ones escape punches.

Ban boxing? If you outlawed it in New York, you'd have fights on barges in the East River. You take two kids fighting in the street, you're going to gather a crowd. For some reason, people want to see one man pitted against another. It's the element of danger we grew up in, especially as a New York kid.

What you have to do is carefully regulate the sport. Make sure the boxers are well taken care of. Boxing's not going to go away, so we better take care of the fighters.

... "YOU'VE HAD ENOUGH, KID...."
—BY BILL GALLO

THE PHILOSOPHER

Fight manager Constantine "Cus" D'Amato told me the thing Floyd Patterson and Mike Tyson and all his other fighters had to understand was fear. He said he didn't want them to get over it. He wanted them to control it, like you control a fire. He always said a fire could burn you, but it also could make you warm.

Under his ever-present homburg, Cus was a philosopher of the ring, the Plato of boxing managers. His last big project was Tyson, but Cus died in 1985, the year before Tyson became champ. Here was my tribute to this pensive kingmaker.

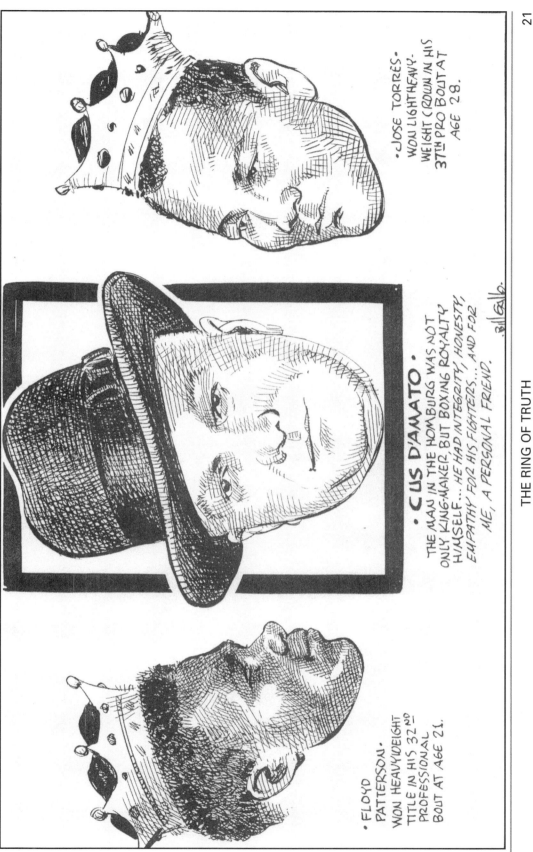

· JOSE TORRES ·
WON LIGHTHEAVY-
WEIGHT CROWN IN HIS
37TH PRO BOUT AT
AGE 28.

· CUS D'AMATO ·
THE MAN IN THE HOMBURG WAS NOT
ONLY KING-MAKER, BUT BOXING ROYALTY
HIMSELF... HE HAD INTEGRITY, HONESTY,
EMPATHY FOR HIS FIGHTERS... AND FOR
ME, A PERSONAL FRIEND.
BillGallo.

· FLOYD
PATTERSON ·
WON HEAVYWEIGHT
TITLE IN HIS 32ND
PROFESSIONAL
BOUT AT AGE 21.

THE EVENT

The first Ali-Frazier fight—March 8, 1971, at Madison Square Garden—was probably the biggest sports event in terms of excitement, anticipation of excitement, that I had ever been to. It totally transcended the sport. In one corner was Muhammad Ali, the former heavyweight champion, stripped of his title and driven into exile for refusing to be drafted into military service during the Vietnam War; in the other corner, Joe Frazier, the reigning champ. Both undefeated as pros. There was such electricity in the crowd. Enough celebrities were present to make it look like an Academy Awards audience. Frank Sinatra was there in the working press, as a photographer; he did an admirable job.

I recalled the clash on its twenty-fifth anniversary, in 1996. It wasn't the greatest fight I've seen. It was a good fight. What made it suspenseful was not knowing whether Joe Frazier was going to knock Ali out.

Ali at the time was considered good, but he wasn't the great, great one that he was considered later. He had been out for three years. We didn't know how well he was going to come back. . . . The boxing elite wouldn't allow him ultimate greatness—yet.

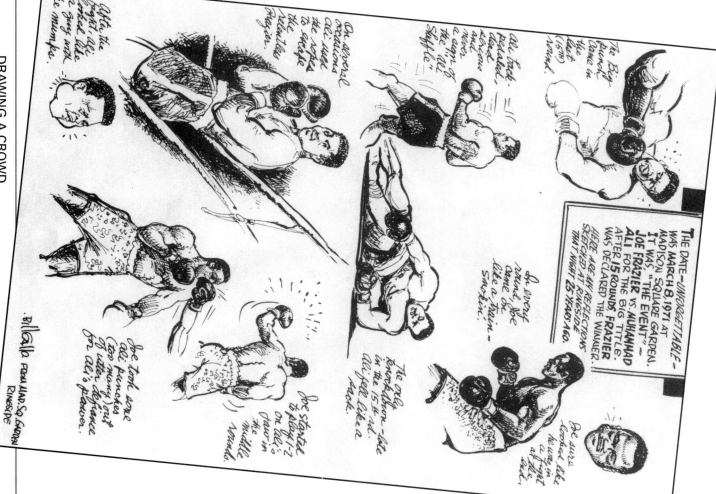

THAT IS THE QUESTION

His first fight with Frazier was a big test for Ali, to see how rusty he had been from the layoff. He did really well, I thought. He lost. Decidedly lost. But he fought admirably. He tried like hell. Joe fought with the determination of a man who was not going to lose. You saw it in every round.

The question I raised in this cartoon—How you gonna whup him?—was about the first Ali-Frazier match. When they met again in the Garden, in January 1974, Ali just boxed his ears off.

KING GEORGE I AND II

There have been two George Foremans. George No. 1 fought Joe Frazier and Ken Norton in the 1970s; he wasn't fond of the press and wasn't cordial with anybody. He seemed to be angry all the time. I thought that demeanor was reserved for Sonny Liston, but George had some of it, too. He was aloof, hard to talk to.

When Foreman reemerged in 1987, after ten years away from the game, he was George No. 2. He was a very pleasant guy. In every way, George No. 2 was the better man—the better businessman, too. He became a preacher, and that might have had something to do with it. There was something troubling the first George, whereas George No. 2 seems to be free, free of all the agony he had, whatever it was.

I juxtaposed the two Georges in the 1990s when he was again going for the title. I used a lot of crosshatching to depict the '70s-era Foreman. Crosshatching is a way to provide shadow and to mold shape, such as in the face. It's an old technique that was employed by editorial cartoonist Thomas Nast in the nineteenth century—but it still works.

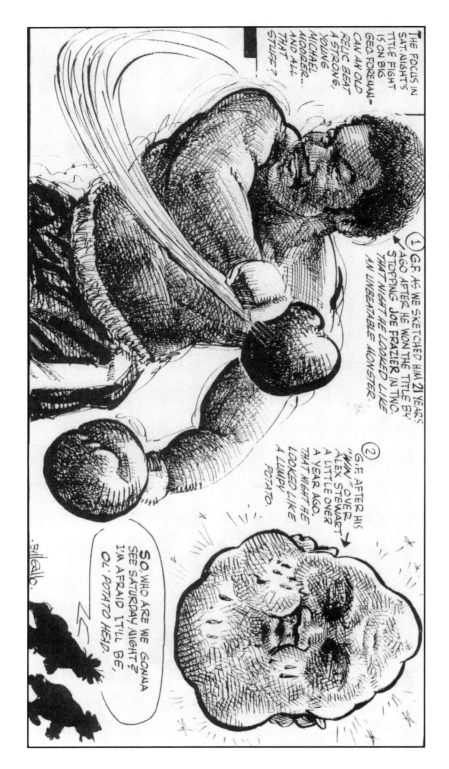

① G.F. AS WE SKETCHED HIM 21 YEARS AGO AFTER HE WON THE TITLE BY STOPPING JOE FRAZIER IN TWO. THAT NIGHT HE LOOKED LIKE AN UNBEATABLE MONSTER.

② G.F. AFTER HIS "WIN" OVER ALEX STEWART A LITTLE OVER A YEAR AGO. THAT NIGHT HE LOOKED LIKE A LUMPY POTATO.

SO WHO ARE WE GONNA SEE SATURDAY NIGHT? I'M AFRAID IT'LL BE, OL' POTATO HEAD.

THE FOCUS IN SAT. NIGHT'S TITLE FIGHT IS ON BIG GEO. FOREMAN—CAN AN OLD RELIC BEAT A STRONG, YOUNG MICHAEL MOORER... AND ALL THAT STUFF?

CROWNING ACHIEVEMENT

Twenty years after George No. 1 lost his heavyweight crown to Muhammad Ali in Zaire, George No. 2 reclaimed it. To mark his triumph, I echoed the "Who's a Bum!" cartoon about the Brooklyn Dodgers of nearly forty years before.

A BLOW TO HIS PRIDE

Born in 1951, Roberto Duran was brought up a poor kid in Panama. He had to steal bread, steal food, when he was eleven and twelve years old. He was a tough street kid, fearless… a great lightweight and welterweight who became champ in both categories. He was one of the best that I've seen.

I drew this in 1980, before Duran's second match with Sugar Ray Leonard, who himself wore a number of crowns during his career. Roberto had won the first contest, but this rematch was to go down in sports history as the "no mas" fight, when Duran walked away from his opponent and gave up. That "no mas" broke the heart of Duran's trainer, Ray Arcel, who loved Roberto like a son (and the feeling was mutual).

Carlos Eleta, Roberto's manager, later told me that Duran felt so guilty about the way that fight ended. He was being beaten, Eleta explained, and Duran didn't want to embarrass himself. He knew he wasn't going to beat Sugar Ray Leonard that night, and he didn't want to be made a fool of. That's the mentality of the streets.

TYSON, TOP TO BOTTOM

On June 27, 1988, Mike Tyson knocked out Michael Spinks in the first round and became undisputed heavyweight champion. After that, it started to go downhill for him. Tyson changed somewhat; his personality changed. It was probably always there, but he started to show a surly side. Right after the Spinks fight, he fired his manager, Bill Cayton, and went to Don King. And he fired his trainer, Kevin Rooney. That's when everything changed for him. I'm not saying his troubles were anybody's fault but Tyson's. I'm just saying it changed for him.

Mike Tyson wasn't the fighter he was even in winning some of his bouts. He lost the enthusiastic herky-jerkiness that he had, that he needed. He lost his great zest for combat. He just wanted to knock out a guy with one punch so he could get out of there. He still looked invincible when I showed Cupid dropping him at the time of his 1988 marriage to actress Robin Givens. My time-bomb image for Tyson dates back to the '80s and the early part of his career.

NEWS ITEM: MIKE TYSON WAS KNOCKED FOR A LOOP YESTERDAY... DELIVERING THE FINISHER, A LEFT HOOK TO THE HEART WAS KID CUPID.

I THOUGHT YOU SAID TYSON COULD TAKE A PUNCH.

NOT THAT KIND!

TYSON

IN MEMORY OF A FRIEND

Next to my father, the man I respected most in my life was Ray Arcel, the great fight trainer of Roberto Duran, Larry Holmes, Ezzard Charles and many other ring champions. Arcel, who died in 1994, was such a gentleman and so honest in such a brutal and sometimes deceiving sport. He was a diamond in the rough. He once told me that to be a manager you have to be a babysitter, trainer and psychiatrist to the fighter, but he also was a philosopher and a teacher. I sketched this portrait of Ray overseeing Duran's training from a photo taken in the 1980s.

In 1998, a bench was placed between 59th and 60th Streets in New York, on the same side as the Plaza Hotel. On the back of the bench are these words:

IN MEMORY OF RAY ARCEL—HIS LEGACY WAS LOVE

It is signed by Stephanie Arcel, his dear wife.

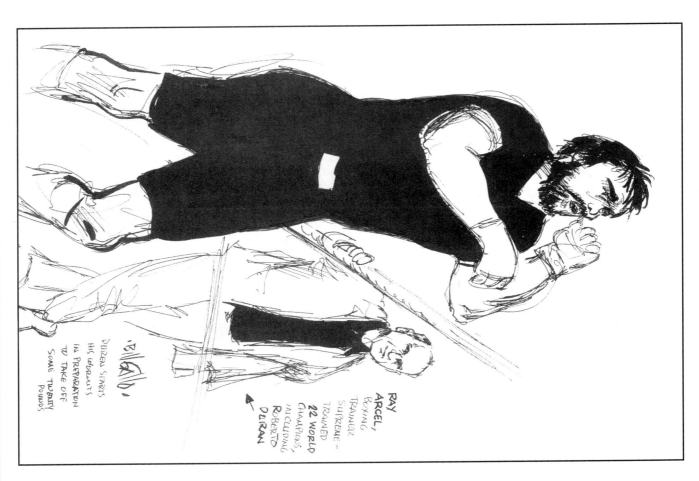

CHAPTER TWO

HAPPY BERTHA-DAY

BASEMENT BERTHA

Basement Bertha was inspired by the cellar-dwelling Mets of the early '60s, particularly the 1962 squad that lost 120 of 160 games. The best way to draw those Mets was to draw Casey Stengel, their first manager.

One day in 1965, for a rainout, I had Casey hanging up his clothes—in the basement, of course—and he was talking to himself. My managing editor, Robert Shand, observed, "You always have Casey alone in the cartoon. The reader questions that. You should have him bounce off somebody. You've got to create a character."

As soon as he said it, I knew he was right. But what character? The image of a bum had already been used for the Brooklyn Dodgers. How about a frumpy female? Not a disgusting one, kind of a pixie. I thought of Sancho Panza in *Don Quixote*. I thought of Yogi Berra, just for the face. I thought of Pearl Bailey, for the personality. I said, "Let me draw this washerwoman who's helping him hang up his clothes."

Shand liked it, told me to do it more, give her a name. I suggested, "Well, they're in the last berth. So we've got Bertha. Why don't we call her Last Place Bertha?" He said, "That's good. The only thing I don't like is 'Last Place.'" But I went with that, and she made her first appearance on June 9, 1965, in the cellar with a space-age Stengel.

Soon after, the mailroom got four letters addressed to "Last Place Bertha," telling her what to advise Casey. From there, Shand shortened it to Basement Bertha, and that was her name a couple of weeks later, when she held Casey's hand and took in the sights at the brand-new Houston Astrodome.

HAPPY BERTHA-DAY

In September 1975, an article in the *New York News Magazine* uncovered the private side of Bertha. Readers learned that she was working as an apartment super in Canarsie, living rent-free in the basement (where else?). Her father was a subway motorman, and she had a sometime boyfriend, Rocco, who would show up at her place with "a six-pack and a bouquet of secondhand flowers."

Bertha was destined for big things, though, and she even had her own comic strip in *The News* in the 1970s. Here she repeats a truism favored by my own mother.

A BEVY OF BERTHA

Our versatile heroine has filled a number of roles over the years. She has served as an authority on baseball and was a symbol of the happy loser when populating the last-place Mets of 1977. Mets exec M. Donald Grant, who oversaw the team's personnel moves, joined Bertha in the team picture.

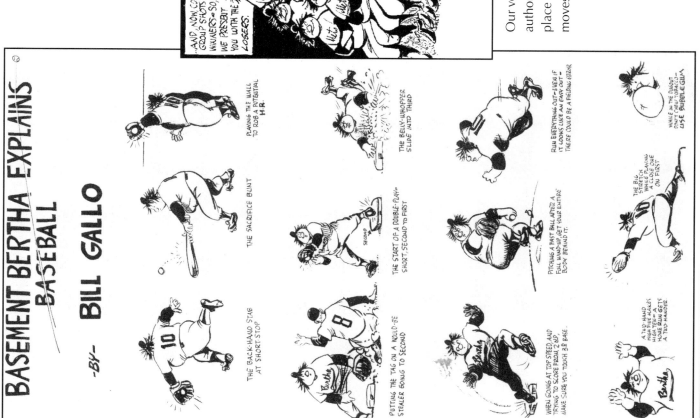

HAPPY BERTHA-DAY

WHAT BECOMES A LEGEND MOST?

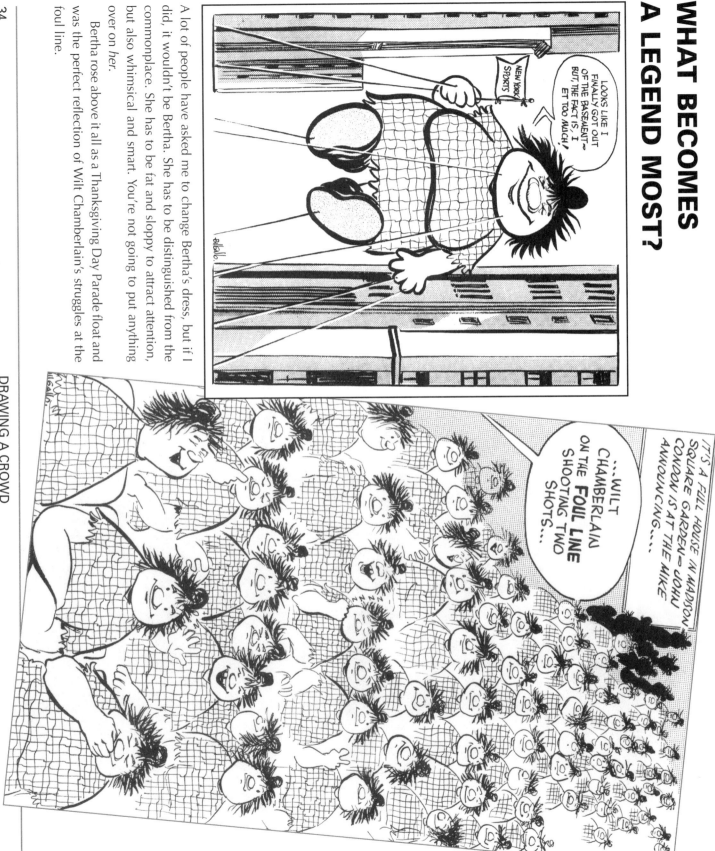

A lot of people have asked me to change Bertha's dress, but if I did, it wouldn't be Bertha. She has to be distinguished from the commonplace. She has to be fat and sloppy to attract attention, but also whimsical and smart. You're not going to put anything over on her.

Bertha rose above it all as a Thanksgiving Day Parade float and was the perfect reflection of Wilt Chamberlain's struggles at the foul line.

AY, THERE'S THE RUB

Bertha was on the fast track to Olympic glory in 1984. Pondering the slings and arrows of outrageous fortune, she wondered if a pennant was to be or not to be for the 1996 Yankees.

HAPPY BERTHA-DAY

UPWARDLY MOBILE

In 1993, I got hold of an invitation to Donald Trump's wedding to Marla Maples at New York's Plaza Hotel. Of course, a person like Bertha is not going to be invited, which is what made it funny—the incongruity of her at The Plaza.

ODDS-ON FAVORITE

Bernie the Bulgarian began as a takeoff on the oddsmaker Jimmy the Greek, who used to pick football games for *The News*. I'd make fun of Jimmy in cartoons, and one day I decided to give him a friend, a guy who can pick football games better than The Greek could. He'll be a good-natured wise guy. I'll make him fat, because fat is funnier than skinny. I decided to call him Bernie, which is close to Bertha. The managing editor, Robert Shand, suggested "The Bulgarian"—we figured there weren't many Bulgarians in New York who could take offense. Besides, that name continued the alliteration I had used with Basement Bertha.

In this 1971 drawing, Bernie explains to The Greek his system for figuring the point spread in Super Bowl V, between the Baltimore Colts and the Dallas Cowboys.

BERNIE THE BULGARIAN—ODDSMAKER

THE GANG'S ALL HERE

Drawing a cartoon is like writing a play: you've got to have characters. Take Penthouse Polly, Bertha's well-off sister. I used her in the illustration at left to show how a few New York coaches had risen in the world. Some characters come in and out. Bertha and Bernie, though, are regulars. And Yuchie. But more about him later . . .

HAPPY BERTHA-DAY

THE EXTENDED GALLO FAMILY

TAE CAST!

Basement Bertha . . . The sports philosopher who doesn't think losing is the end of the world.

Bernie the Bulgarian . . . The oddsmaker who is wise enough not to be taken in by the "smart guys."

Yuchie . . . The perennial youth in all of us.

Sunshine Sam . . . The kind of fellow who always sees the bright side; his glass is half full.

Gloomy Gus . . . The downer who sees everybody losing; his glass is half empty.

The Brain . . . Every class in grammar school had a kid like this. One of those boys grew up to be Bill Gates.

General Von Steingrabber . . . A fun character who closely resembles George Steinbrenner—in spirit, that is.

Penthouse Polly . . . Bertha's older sister who struck it rich.

Professor Bigschmartz . . . The guy we go to when there's serious figuring to do, batting averages included. He's as smart as Einstein, and that's why he looks like him.

Blayfrab and Lunard . . . Products of the space program and the race to get to the moon, these two creatures are way out.

Johnny Unda . . . A friend of the underdog. Truth be told, he is modeled after yours truly.

CHAPTER THREE

MANTLE AND MARIS ON HIGHWAY 61

AN EPIC FOR THE AGES

One of the exciting chapters in baseball history was the race between Roger Maris and Mickey Mantle to hit 61 home runs. Their rivalry was a huge event, bigger than the Mark McGwire–Sammy Sosa duel of 1998, because it was the first real threat to Ruth's record. The 60 home runs belted by the Babe in 1927 had been considered unreachable. Ruth himself was said to remark: "Let's see some son of a bitch beat that one." A couple of sluggers came close—Hank Greenberg, Jimmie Foxx—but couldn't quite do it. Then came 1961 . . .

THIS COULD BE ANOTHER CLASSIC!

HOMER'S ODYSSEY

19 61

MANTLE-MARIS INC. PUBLISHERS

MORE POWER TO 'EM

While both Mantle and Maris were heavy hitters in the Yankee lineup, Mickey was the fan favorite. If anybody was going to have the gall to break Ruth's record, the thinking went, let it be Mantle, widely regarded as the heir apparent. It was okay for Mantle, not okay for Maris, and that's why they got on Roger so much. They didn't believe that he could, or should, do it.

MANTLE AND MARIS ON HIGHWAY 61

IN ISOLATION

Mantle figured to overtake Ruth that year, then Mickey developed a hip injury and some of the interest in the race waned. Mantle had been the sweetheart; Maris, while a nice guy, was so reticent.

MARIS BY THE NUMBERS

I have such admiration for Roger Maris. He broke that record under such pressure—pressure he wasn't accustomed to and didn't want. Other guys could take that pressure and enjoy it. But Maris just wanted to be a ballplayer, a good ballplayer. Here, Bertha and I recount his record-setting season, building a portrait out of the dates he hit his home runs and the pitchers who yielded them.

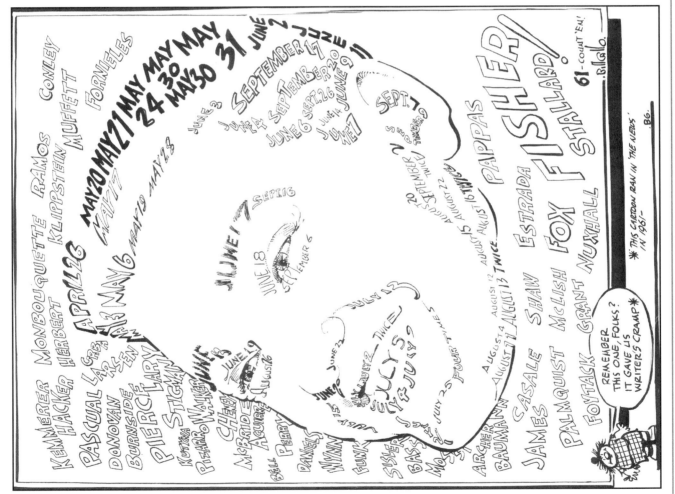

*THIS CARTOON RAN IN THE NEWS' IN 1961

CURTAIN CALL

The last time I saw Roger was in 1985. It was at the Waldorf, and he was to receive the Pride of the Yankees Award at the team's homecoming dinner. *The News* was involved in all these dinners, and I was to present Roger with our Front Page Award.

It was good to see him, but what he told me nearly knocked me off my chair. We were seated next to one another, and while in conversation, he calmly informed me: "I won't be making this dinner next year, because I'm dying of cancer." He stated it like "Tomorrow's Tuesday."

He was fifty-one at the time, and he died before the year was out. He was one of the fine people I was privileged to meet in sports.

DRAWING A CROWD

COMING UP SEVENS

Mickey Mantle was an Oklahoma farm boy, a lovable hayseed. First time I drew him, it was with a hunk of wheat coming out of his ear. He never was really a New Yorker. He was out of his league in the big city. He was uncomfortable—not in the ballpark, but socially, walking the streets of New York. He never felt that he belonged, even afterward, when he had Mickey Mantle's restaurant in Manhattan.

I saw him just before he got sick in the mid-'90s. I sat down with him at Mickey Mantle's and we talked. He was still uncomfortable. . . . . Oh, he did everything with a smile and was pleasant, but there was that underlying uncomfortableness about him. You didn't have to be a psychiatrist to figure it out. You saw it. That's why he hung around with Whitey Ford, who was a city boy. He called Whitey "Slick." Billy Martin was more or less a city boy, too, although he came from California. Mickey

Mantle hung around with these guys so that a little bit of New York would rub off on him.

When Mantle announced his retirement in March 1969, Mickey's No. 7 seemed a fitting way to outline his Yankee career. In 1995, as Mick's health faded, the mood was somber as Mantle fans of all ages hoped for one last rally.

MICKEY GETS THE NOD

Toward the end of his career, Mickey's home-run total was the stuff of dreams, and by 1974 both Mantle and teammate Whitey Ford were en route to Cooperstown. The Mr. Kerr in the cartoon refers to Baseball Hall of Fame president Paul Kerr.

The Sequel: *McGwire on I-70, Sosa's Route 66*

BIG MAC

Thirteen years after Babe Ruth died, Roger Maris came along and broke the Babe's record. In 1998, thirteen years after Roger Maris died, his record was shattered by both Mark McGwire of the Cardinals and the Cubs' Sammy Sosa, who hit 70 and 66 home runs respectively. As this drawing shows, McGwire also faced naysayers, but he could take it better than Maris. He might have learned from Roger, reading about it. Then again, the press was largely rooting for McGwire, whereas it was unaccepting of Maris. By 1998, the media were welcoming somebody to break the record, and we had two of them.

MANTLE AND MARIS ON HIGHWAY 61

McGwire did have to answer for his use of Androstenedione, a legal drug used by bodybuilders. This was fair game, and I had fun with something

that was a fact. I wasn't suggesting that the pills were responsible for his success. I was only commenting on the fact was he was taking them.

MORE POWER TO HIM

I also tipped my cap to McGwire in the drawing below, which incorporates the Cardinals' logo of two redbirds perched atop a bat.

SLAMMIN' SAMMY

You didn't have to be starry-eyed to predict that Sammy Sosa, the pride of the Dominican Republic, would be the National League MVP for 1998. While McGwire hit more home runs, Sosa's Cubs qualified for the post-season, making this one of the safer forecasts.

CHAPTER FOUR

MIRROR, MIRROR ON THE WALL

THE INFLATED EGO

Ego is sometimes considered a dirty word, but it's not. Egos can be good. The big names in sports often have to have big egos. It's when it gets to be "me, me, me" that it gets boring.

With some people, like George Steinbrenner or

Donald Trump, the egos are so huge, you know you're not going to hurt them. Some are even flattered by the attention. You pick only on people who are big. All you do is create the needle. They create the gas in the balloon.

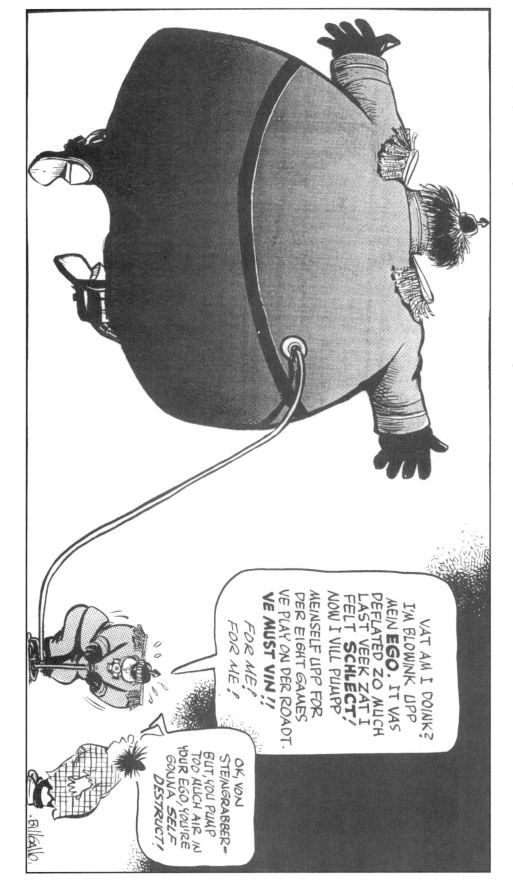

GENERAL-LY SPEAKING

Yankees owner George Steinbrenner has the biggest ego I've ever known. And I certainly have put a needle to that. Better still, he's enjoyed it. People told me constantly that he was mad at me, but he never was. He introduced himself to my wife by saying, "Hello, Mrs. Gallo. I'm General Von Steingrabber."

Here are a couple of my takes on The Boss, including one from the mid-'90s, after the Yankees signed former Mets stars Darryl Strawberry and Dwight Gooden.

MIRROR, MIRROR ON THE WALL

THE BOSS IS ALWAYS RIGHT

Yankee Stadium holds many thousands of fans, but was it big enough for the egos of both five-time Yankee manager Billy Martin and George Steinbrenner?

Billy Martin's personality fell into a different category, defensive rather than self-admiring. Using our amateur psychiatrist's couch, I'd say he was terrifically insecure. It showed in that he had to fight, had to bully people, had to beat them, had to throw that first punch. He learned how to fight from the neighborhood, where you throw the first punch and throw the guy off.

He was what I call a Stirrer—he made things happen. He was one of the first sports figures to regularly invade the front pages of the paper, because of his antics as manager of the Yankees—his firings, his fistfight with a marshmallow salesman, a near-fistfight with Reggie Jackson, his battles with Steinbrenner.

DON'T MESS WITH BILLY

THE DRESS UP BILLY MARTIN GAME
(ANYBODY CAN PLAY)

JACK DANIELS AND SODA

WRITE IN A TEAM (ANY TEAM)

EVERLAST

KID GLOVES

IF YOU FEEL HE'S TIRED OF ALL THIS, SIT HIM DOWN ON A BAR STOOL

1980 PENNANT

World Champions 1977

REGGIE

RETURN ENGAGEMENT

There's an element of show business in all of sports, and Martin and Steinbrenner actually put on an act in front of the TV cameras: "You're fired." "No, I'm not." "Yes, you are." It would wind up like a vaudeville gag, unrehearsed. Then there was Martin's return from exile to again manage the Yanks, which I humorously likened to General MacArthur's return to the Philippines in World War II.

You had to admire Billy for his leadership quality. He knew the game, knew what he wanted and was tough. He was a winner. Not in his personal life. On the field.

THREE'S A CROWD

Reggie Jackson was another tremendous ego on those late '70s and early '80s Yankees. The star outfielder didn't do anything quietly or anonymously, from his Reggie candy bar to his reputation as "the straw that stirs the drink." He also had his differences with Martin, and Billy's return as manager in 1979 triggered a war of words between Jackson and Steinbrenner. This illustration from September 1979, titled "Me, Myself and I," is from that very public feud between Reggie and The Boss.

TOYING WITH AN IDEA

Donald Trump moves primarily in real-estate circles, but he did own the New Jersey Generals of the old United States Football League and presented some of Mike Tyson's fights. Plus his ego is as big as Trump Tower.

I placed him in a playpen in the '80s, when it was rumored that he wanted to become Tyson's manager in place of Bill Cayton. But Trump told me he wasn't interested in getting into the boxing business. He just wanted to host Tyson's bouts,

particularly in Atlantic City. So I scoffed at the rumor with this illustration, and Donald got a kick out of it.

LIP SERVICE

Leo "The Lip" Durocher was a flamboyant guy, a performer. He acted like a celebrity, hung around with all the stars, and was a friend of Sinatra. Durocher had an admirer in Bertha, too, who cre- ated his likeness when he was managing the Cubs. Her "broad daylight" reference is to when the Cubs played all their home games in the day, before lights were finally installed at Wrigley Field.

BEARS REPEATING

The Lip was famous for saying, "Nice guys finish last," which came back to haunt him in 1969 when his Cubs were overtaken by the Miracle Mets, managed by a nice guy, Gil Hodges. To mark that turn of events, I put Leo in a dunce cap and had him recite his lesson.

I once asked Durocher if he had actually said that remark about nice guys, and all he did was smile. By that time, he owned the saying. It's repeated so many times, the person owns it.

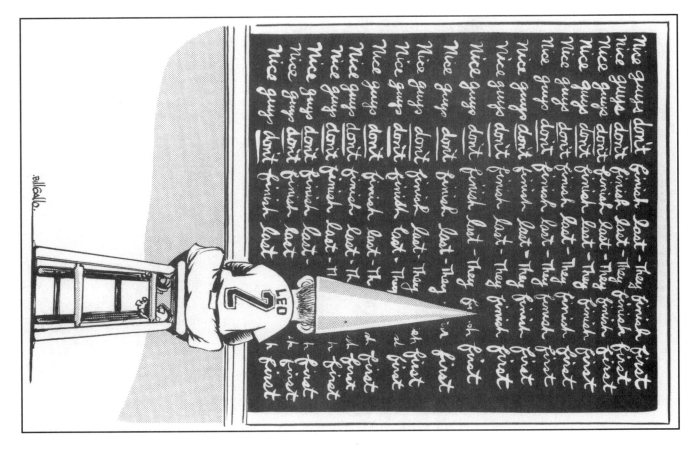

CLOSEMOUTHED

When Ali lost to Frazier in 1971, I zipped his lips in an illustration that still makes the rounds. But that wasn't the first time this drawing ran in the *Daily News*. It had appeared five years earlier, amid the growing furor over Ali's stand against the Vietnam War. He had already declared, "I ain't got no quarrel with the Viet Cong" while training for a bout with Ernie Terrell. The fight was to be in Chicago, and in the ensuing controversy Ali appeared before the Illinois Athletic Commission to explain himself. He refused to apologize to the commission, which prompted my cartoon under the heading "Enough Already!" That was the way I felt in 1966. A few years later, I would come around to Ali's point of view.

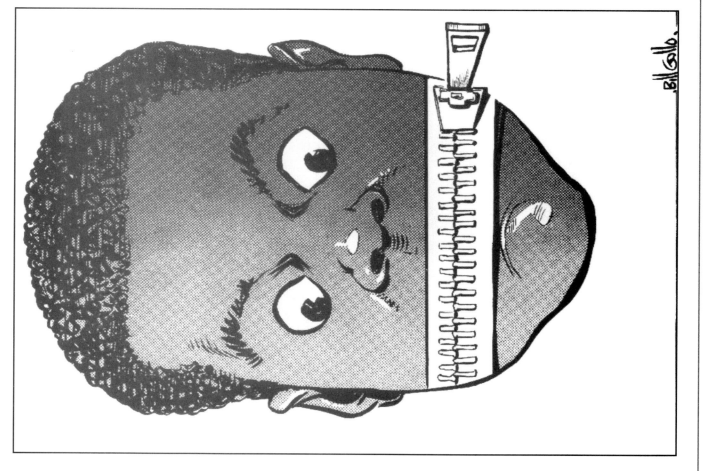

MIRROR, MIRROR ON THE WALL

HE CARRIED WEIGHT

I drew an overweight Ali carting around his stomach on the occasion of his (brief) retirement in 1979. "You know, Gallo, you did me a favor drawing that cartoon showing me with that fat belly resting in a wheelbarrow," Ali told me the following year while training to fight Larry Holmes. "That cartoon was hung in my training camp in Deer Lake [Pennsylvania], and I looked at it every day and it supplied the inspiration for me to trim down."

Ali lost that bout and his bid to be heavyweight champ a fourth time, but to this day Muhammad greets me by making a semicircular motion in front of his stomach.

CHAPTER FIVE

WHEN LOMBARDI GOT STEAMED

MOUNT LOMBARDI

Vince Lombardi is remembered today as the fiercely competitive, no-nonsense coach of those great Green Bay Packer teams of the 1960s, an intimidating figure who wouldn't tolerate losing. But the Lombardi I knew could be downright gregarious.

I'd had an admiration and respect for Lombardi, for his leadership, before I ever knew him. So I started to draw him, and I labeled him "Mount Lombardi," because to me he was a mountain of a man. I carved him into Mount Rushmore (along with Casey Stengel) and cast him as a towering obstacle to Oakland Raiders quarterback Daryle Lamonica in the second Super Bowl, won by Green Bay in January 1968.

WINNING WAYS

Then I got to meet Lombardi, and we hit it off. He was a different man from the one I'd read about. Socially, he was kind of a fun-loving guy. I chuckled at the way he relished his own jokes, with his big old laugh and gap-toothed smile. He told good, clean jokes because priests were frequently in his presence. He had wanted to be a priest himself.

Lombardi used to hold court at The New York Athletic Club; his "Knights of the Baths" would meet in a private steam room. I was lucky to be invited once with John Condon, the longtime announcer for Madison Square Garden. Lombardi introduced us to the men there, middle-aged guys and old guys, Mr. So-and-So, Mr. So-and-So, always with a smile, as if he was getting a kick out of introducing us. The people were very pleasant, and we chatted. Good conversation.

I had assumed they were big-time businessmen, but when we got dressed, I noticed that all these old men were putting on collars. Most of them were priests! That was Lombardi's pixieish sense of humor.

Lombardi's wife, Marie, would request all the drawings that I did of him, and I did quite a few. This one was her favorite.

WHEN LOMBARDI GOT STEAMED

VINTAGE VINCE

Perhaps because his father made wine, Vince himself was partial to one of my drawings that depicted him as a winemaker tending to his Packer veterans. I drew it in early 1967, after Green Bay beat the Dallas Cowboys to win the NFL championship and advance to the first Super Bowl. I also showed a jovial Lombardi about to feast on the Giants in October 1967, but first placing a side order with a restaurateur.

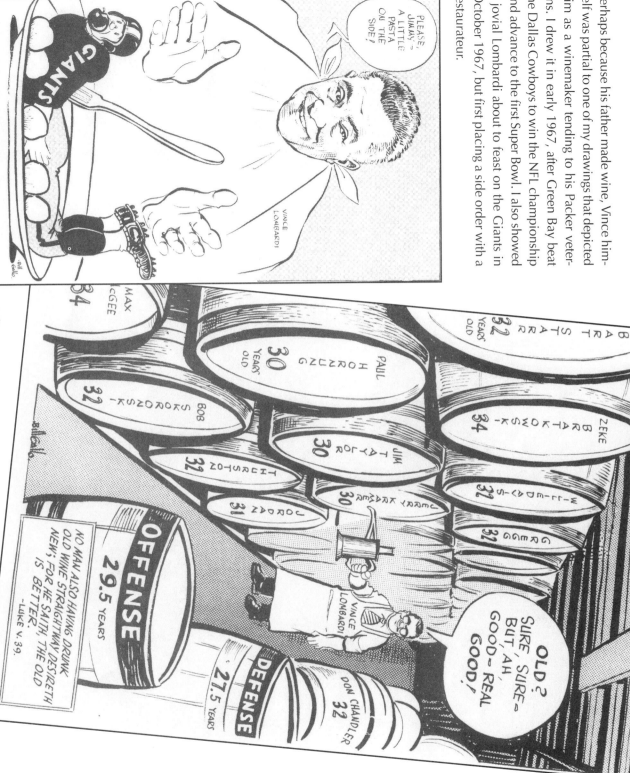

A ROARING SUCCESS

In the locker room after games, he was the Lombardi you read about. Once he turned *News* sports columnist Dick Young upside down, gave him a real bawling out over a question Young had asked. Dick usually didn't take anything from anybody, but he did from Lombardi.

When Lombardi was like that, I stayed away from him, although I drew on that side of him in my illustrations. One cartoon gave a taste of the "Demanding One" before a big game with the Rams in 1967; when the Packers lost that contest, I had him literally taking a player's head off. Green Bay, incidentally, did rebound that season to win another title.

WHEN LOMBARDI GOT STEAMED

THE 'SKINS GAME

An eager-beaver reporter stumbled into the teeth of Lombardi's fury in the 1968 drawing at right, as Vince announced that he was stepping down as coach of the Packers but staying on as general manager. A year later he would leave the team altogether, to lead the Washington Redskins; I illustrated this new, and ultimately final, chapter in a monumental career.

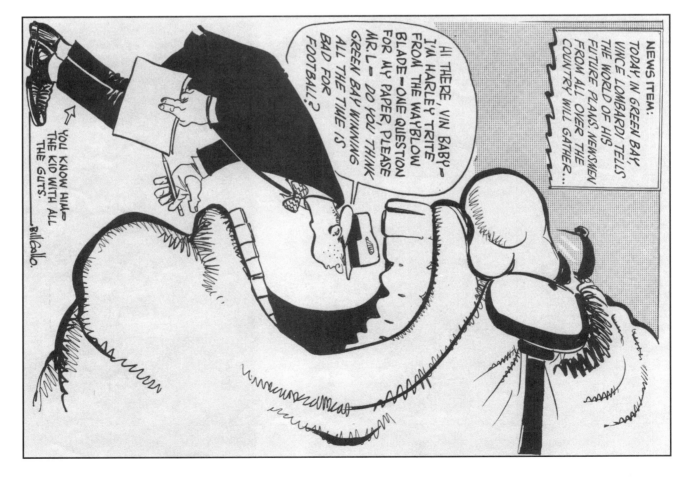

GLOWER POWER

Lombardi was a tough act to follow in Green Bay, and my suggestion to Phil Bengston, his successor as Packer coach, was to don Vince's game face.

WHEN LOMBARDI GOT STEAMED

LOMBARDI AT HIS PEAK

Did he really say, "Winning isn't everything—it's the only thing"? I don't think he put it that way. Lombardi said a lot more valid things than that. In my presence, he never acknowledged that. It came up once or twice. He didn't respond, "*I didn't say that.*" It wasn't like that. But he never admitted it.

Here's how I marked Vince's passing, from cancer, in September 1970. He was fifty-seven.

CHAPTER SIX

THE OLD NEIGHBORHOOD

BATTER UP!

Every neighborhood has an athlete who stands out. He can do everything, excels at every sport. The kid who excelled in our neighborhood was named Yuchie—pronounced YOU-chee, an Italian diminutive for Eugene. He was a tremendous ballplayer. He could pitch; he could hit. He was the best football player, and when we played roller hockey, he was tops there, too.

Then World War II started, and Yuchie went into the Navy. He was killed at the Battle of Midway. He was eighteen years old.

When I started drawing little kids playing ball, I thought of Yuchie and I used him to represent the kid in all of us. I wasn't trying to make a shrine to him. In my cartoons, he became the epitome of youngsters. Everybody wants to be a Yuchie; this guy is like we all were, or wanted to be.

DIAMONDS ARE FOREVER

I often include Yuchie in my feature "Two Kids Talkin' Sports," in which a pair of youngsters finds the simple truths in a variety of situations. In these two cartoons, they're on the baseball field—a place I loved to be when I was growing up. There was no such thing as Little League then, but our season was just as organized. We ran our own clubs, playing other neighborhood teams on the ample sandlot ballfields of Astoria. The home team would pass around the hat after the fourth inning; the dimes, quarters and sometimes paper money from generous fans paid for our uniforms.

Our club's name was the Astoria Pirates. We weren't bad, but there were sandlot teams that were more advanced, and these brought out the major-league scouts. They saw a few good ones there: Whitey Ford, from the 34th Avenue Boys Club; Billy Loes, who went on to pitch for the Brooklyn Dodgers; and Sam Mele, an exceptional Astoria athlete who wound up playing for the Boston Red Sox (where he hit .302 as a rookie) and later managing the Minnesota Twins to the 1965 World Series.

THE OLD NEIGHBORHOOD

WE HAD A BALL

When I was a kid, the streets of New York were my playground. People who owned cars were the exception, not the rule, and that left the streets open for belting a ten-cent pink rubber Spaldeen ball with a stickball bat (some mom in the neighborhood was a broom handle short) and sending it two manhole covers' distance. Or we might chalk up a big V-shaped field on the asphalt and play Triangle Ball, a kind of simplified, one-on-one stickball.

Remember One-o'-Cat, where you would toss the Spaldeen up in the air yourself and hit it, all in one motion, toward a single fielder? He either caught it on the fly or fielded the grounder and rolled it toward your bat, now placed on the ground. If he hit it, you were out—but wait: you had to catch it when it bounced off the stick.

War would break out from time to time—the game of War, that is. Kids would stand in marked-off areas or "countries" and try to avoid being hit. Otherwise, you would be "it."

We would scatter during Ring-a-Levio, a team hide-and-seek game in which players were captured and rescued, and gather for Association, sort of one-hand touch football using a rolled-up newspaper. Who owned an actual football?

FOR ALL THE MARBLES

Some forces were beyond our control. A "Jonah" was a guy who put the hex on everything, and sometimes it worked. A "Hindu" was an on-field obstruction—like someone's kid sister—that got in the way of the game and was grounds for a do-over.

Marbles, or "immies," was a world unto itself. Flawless "purees" were highly coveted; "steelies," as the name suggested, were industrial-strength metallic marbles that could shatter the whole pot. And there was always the kid with his cheesebox with holes cut out; he'd give you odds on shooting a marble into a particular hole for a payoff, but usually went home with the immies. Let's face it—this kid was a born bookmaker.

THE OLD NEIGHBORHOOD

WHEN JOSH CONNECTED

We kids would go to Queens Park sometimes to see the Homestead Grays in action. They were a marvelous band of black athletes who could play the game of baseball like nobody's business. Way beyond the center-field fence were railroad tracks, where no one ever managed to hit one. No one, that is, except the Grays' Josh Gibson, the legendary slugger who was said to have hit 84 home runs in a single season. Whenever the Grays would come to Queens Park, the fans would cheer for Gibson to hit one to the tracks, just so they could say they'd seen it. I can say I saw it once myself.

Jackie Robinson hadn't come along yet, so Josh never was allowed into the major leagues. But he did make it to the Hall of Fame in 1972, twenty-five years after his death. That's when I recalled a boy's-eye view of that great ballplayer.

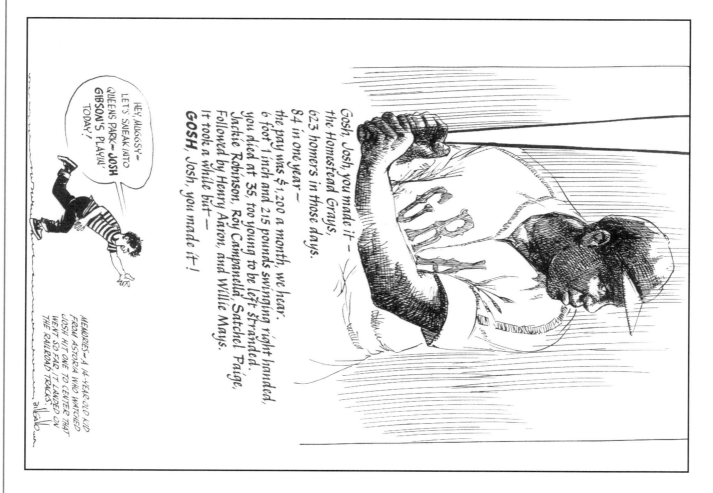

Gosh, Josh, you made it —
the Homestead Grays,
623 homers in those days.
84 in one year —
the pay was $1,200 a month, we hear.
6 foot 1 inch and 215 pounds swinging right-handed,
you died at 35, too young to be left stranded.
Jackie Robinson, Roy Campanella, Satchel Paige,
Followed by Henry Aaron, and Willie Mays.
It took a while but —
GOSH, Josh, you made it!

HEY, MUGGSY —
LET'S SNEAK INTO
QUEENS PARK — JOSH
GIBSON'S PLAYIN'
TODAY!

MEMORIES — A 14-YEAR-OLD KID
FROM ASTORIA WHO WATCHED
JOSH HIT ONE TO CENTER THAT
WENT SO FAR IT LANDED ON
THE RAILROAD TRACKS.

ATTENTION: DADS

I frequently include a message to dads in my cartoons: Get off the couch and have a catch with your kid. There's a reason for this. After my own dad died, I missed that father figure with whom I could have a catch. It was gone, gone.

I'd look across the street, to a friend of mine named Billy Bachman. He and his father hardly talked to one another, but the one thing they did together was have a catch. It was like their own two-man secret society. They'd be right across the street, and I'd watch from my window and wonder, "Gee, why don't they ask me to have a catch?" It was just the lament of a little boy, but it meant something to me.

The cartoon below is from Father's Day 1993, but I don't need a holiday to remind dads: "It's Sunday. Have a catch with your kid today. Don't forget to have that catch with your kid."

I've gotten a lot of letters on that.

CHAPTER SEVEN

DODGING FAME: SANDY KOUFAX

AHEAD OF THE CURVE

Early in his career, Sandy Koufax couldn't get the ball over the plate. The Dodgers knew that he had something. It was just that he had no control. There was another pitcher like that: Rex Barney. They compared Koufax to Barney—a lot of talent but no control.

Koufax was one of those men who worked hard as hell, about as hard as Bob Feller did. Years back, Bob Feller would throw and throw and throw. That's what Koufax did. Sandy Koufax, to me, was the epitome of a champion.

TAKING CONTROL

Koufax was the DiMaggio of pitchers. He had to get it right—the perfectionist. A pitcher wants to "paint" the corners of the plate, just nick the strike zone, and Koufax was almost mathematical about cutting the plate's corners.

What was his biggest enemy, control, became his best friend, great control. The guy became unhittable, phenomenal. For two or three years, he was absolutely the greatest pitcher who ever lived. It was amazing what a great pitcher he was. He was right up there, doing his thing, with DiMag. With Sinatra. With Fred Astaire. With Picasso. It's when nobody can do it any better, before or since. Koufax was showing his dominance during the 1963 season when my cartoon "Sandy, You're a Dandy," appeared.

Sandy, You're a Dandy —— by Gallo

WON 15 LOST 3

WORKED 165 INNINGS

ALLOWED 99 HITS

ISSUED 35 WALKS

9 SHUTOUTS

NO-HITTER VS. GIANTS MAY 11, 1963

163 STRIKE OUTS

ERA 1.64

PUTTING THE K
IN KOUFAX

I marveled at Sandy's 15-strikeout performance against the Yankees in the opening game of the 1963 World Series. The title, "KKKKKKKKKKKKKKKool, Man," was spelled, fittingly, with 15 Ks.

Writing about the game the next day, *The News'* Joe Trimble marveled: "The Yankees thought Sandy Koufax was human. 'Taint so. The Dodgers' great lefthander is a pitching machine."

A PLACE IN HISTORY

In 1998, I ran into Sandy at a benefit celebrity golf tournament. He appeared the same in stature and figure, lean and serious-looking. He was reticent and shy as always, not wanting to bother with too many people. We talked over a cup of coffee, and he loosened up a bit. The conversation at first was about baseball in his time, but he politely let me know that it's not his favorite topic.

I said, "Sandy, I have a lot of clippings of box scores, pictures, and some cartoons of you when you were playing. I'd be glad to give them to you. Would you like me to send them?"

His response startled me. He put out his hand as if to signal stop and said, "Please, no. I don't want them. In fact, I'm in the process of getting rid of all the things I already have."

He said it with no bitterness. On the contrary, he was extremely pleasant and made an effort to explain. "That baseball pitcher people saw many years ago was somebody else," he said. "You do that in one part of your life and you go on. I don't look back."

That explanation reminded me of what Fred Astaire once said when asked, long after he had hung up his dancing shoes, if he watched his old movies with Ginger Rogers. "Never," replied the dapper old guy with a half-smile. "Who wants to look at that again? It's over, something I once did and that's all. Finished. Forgotten about."

Suddenly I thought that here are two people, the very best in their fields, not knowing one another but saying the same thing.

The "Cooperstown, U.S.A." drawing captured Sandy at a flawless peak, after he threw his perfect game in 1965, a 1-0 victory over the Chicago Cubs. He took no chances at the end—he struck out the side in both the eighth and ninth innings.

DODGING FAME: SANDY KOUFAX

GOING, GOING, GONE

By the time Koufax had developed into a dominant pitcher, the Dodgers were gone from Brooklyn. Owner Walter O'Malley had taken the franchise to Los Angeles (and talked Horace Stoneham into moving the New York Giants to San Francisco) after the 1957 season. A cartoon of mine from that October looks at the team's departure and sees the glass as half full, reasoning that New Yorkers still had the Rangers in hockey. I drew this while apprenticing under Leo O'Mealia, *The News'* first-string sports cartoonist, and the style of this illustration is strictly Leo's. It's not my greatest effort, admittedly a bit crude, but I was desperately trying to win the approval of managing editor Robert Shand and land a cartoonist's job.

MONEY BAGS

Brooklyn diehards never forgave O'Malley, but that seemed like a waste of time. In the grand scheme of things, he wasn't a very important man. When the thing you're most remembered for is moving a team, that's not much.

I could feel for the Brooklyn fan, but I could also see why O'Malley did it. It came down to money, and O'Malley was a businessman, not a baseball man. Today, we recognize it as a money game, but we didn't then.

In O'Malley, I saw the figure of the perennial landlord during the Depression. That's the way I drew him, and made references to him busily tabulating his riches. This 1968 cartoon has O'Malley relishing the lucrative prospect of National League expansion the following year.

GENTLEMEN, THE THING ABOUT EXPANSION IS THAT WE SURELY ALL FATTEN-UP BY IT!

O'Malley

HE'S REALLY NOT THIS FAT ANYMORE—HE HAS ON HIS MONEY BELT.

THE HOLLYWOOD ENDING

The Dodgers' Bum of Willard Mullin became obsolete when the team left Brooklyn. In my drawings, he was transformed into the Hollywood wanna-be—an amateur in beret, sunglasses and, à la O'Malley, a cigar holder.

For a while, *The News* picked on the Dodgers as if they were still part of the equation in New York. We wanted to tell O'Malley he did the wrong thing, at least by Gotham. It got kind of Johnny One-Note, though, and wore out. Then the Mets came along in 1962—I drew this the following year when the two teams met in the Polo Grounds— and soon we didn't have to worry about Walter O'Malley anymore.

CHAPTER EIGHT

INSPIRED BY THE CLASSICS

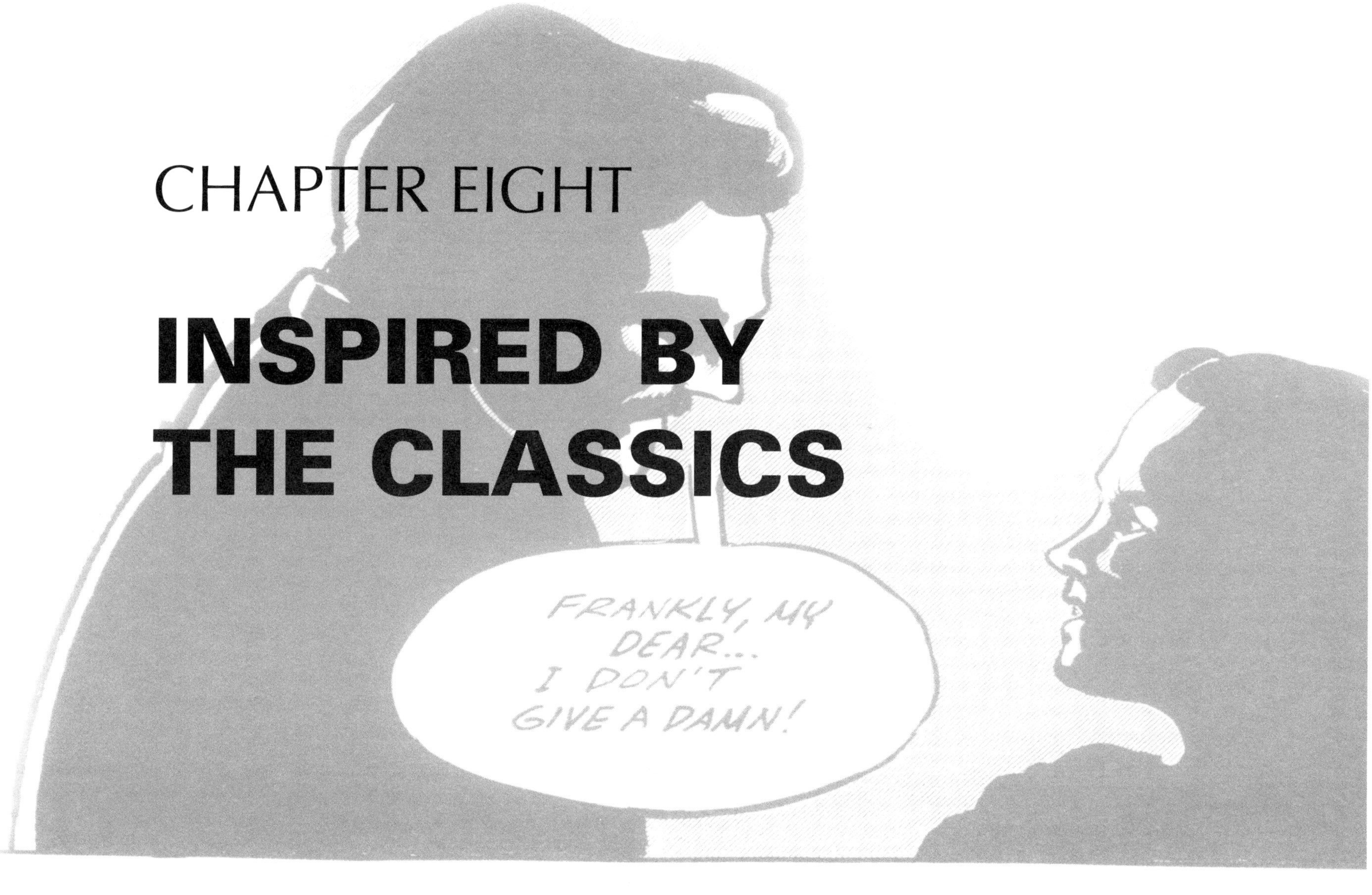

THE IMPOSSIBLE DREAMER

Since you can relate sports to anything, why not to the classics? These are lasting things, they stick to your ribs, and the reader understands the connection almost immediately. Amid a hardball strike in 1981, for example, optimistic baseball commissioner Bowie Kuhn made a fine Don Quixote, with Bertha a natural as Sancho Panza. (The baseball strike, by the way, continued for three weeks more.)

Artists like Picasso and my hero, Goya, have certainly made a lasting impression on me. When I go to Spain—and I have visited there every year since 1962—I spend a lot of time at the Prado in Madrid. Goya has a couple of rooms there, and I tell my wife, "Let's visit my friend Goya." He's influenced me in my use of hard lines, the bold black; he was very sure and direct. Not that I can draw like Goya, but when I draw I seem to think of him.

THE FRENCH CONNECTION

I've always appreciated artists who can use black in their drawings to add impact, to give the work pop. That's why I've always liked Milton Caniff, of "Terry and the Pirates" fame, and the late British cartoonist David Low. I've long admired Bill Mauldin, the war artist, who gave us Willie and Joe. He drew a sure way—nothing fancy, nothing frilly, but he conveyed everything. I also admire Charles Schulz, because he was a philosopher. There's so much intelligence in "Peanuts." It gives you a picture of our time, through kids.

I guess there's a philosophy in any kind of art. There has to be. You can't just draw pictures. Drawing pictures is a nice thing, but guys in the park can draw your portrait for a few bucks. I'm not putting that down, but to be a newspaperman you have to have more than pictures. That's why I invoked the image of Napoleon's retreat from Russia to convey the futility of sports strikes in general and the 1974 football walkout in particular.

LIKE NAPOLEON LEADING HIS BEDRAGGLED TROOPS BACK FROM RUSSIA IN 1812, EDGARVEY, THE PLAYERS' UNION LEADER, RETURNS FROM THE WARS.

TRAINING CAMPS

STEINBECK MEETS STEINBRENNER

How do I get my references? I read a lot. I like biographies; I don't go much for fiction. I'm more interested in the people I'm reading about than the way a book is written. I like a simple kind of writing, which is tough to do. I love James Michener, because his writing is so simple yet explains everything.

Analogies are there for everyone to use. Politics seizes on sports expressions all the time: "Three strikes, you're out." "It was a knockout." "He's a lightweight." I figure if some readers aren't familiar with the references, they're smart enough to look them up or ask somebody who does know. And when a reader says to me, "Why didn't I think of that?" I consider it a high compliment.

I took dramatic license when I likened Billy Martin and George Steinbrenner to Lennie and George from Steinbeck's *Of Mice and Men*. After all, Martin wasn't a dunce, although he did kind of cater to The Boss.

AN HONEST DAY'S WORK

Bart Giamatti, a scholar and former president of Yale, could have been one of the great baseball commissioners if he had not died mere months into his tenure. This cartoon, drawn in 1989 during baseball's investigation of gambling allegations against Pete Rose, showed my appreciation of his honesty. He, in turn, told me of his fondness for the cartoon.

INSPIRED BY THE CLASSICS

OF KNEE I SING

Joe Namath's fragile knees were a constant source of concern to the press and fans during his time with the Jets. It became a real challenge to find a fresh approach to the topic. Then I hit on Joyce Kilmer's "Trees" and thought, instead of tree, why not knee? It gave a familiar cadence to the spoof of all this anxiety and conveyed my exhaustion with the topic.

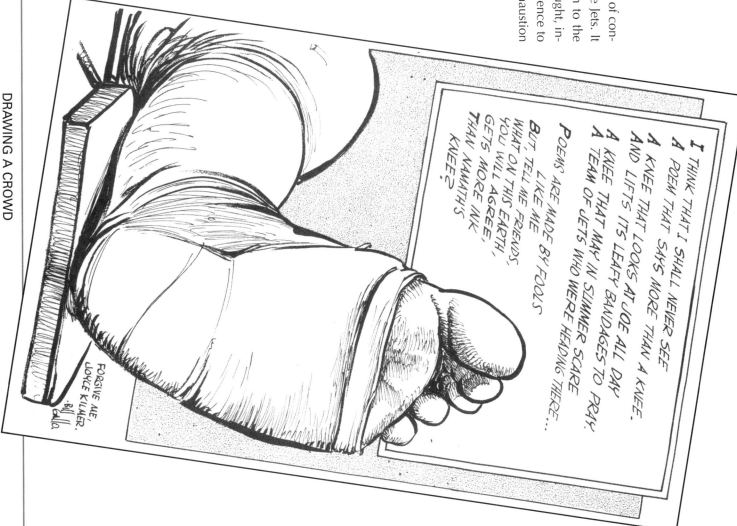

I THINK THAT I SHALL NEVER SEE
A POEM THAT SAYS MORE THAN A KNEE.

A KNEE THAT LOOKS AT JOE ALL DAY
AND LIFTS ITS LEAFY BANDAGES TO PRAY.

A KNEE THAT MAY IN SUMMER SCARE
A TEAM OF JETS WHO WERE HEADING THERE...

POEMS ARE MADE BY FOOLS
LIKE ME

BUT, TELL ME FRIENDS,
WHAT ON THIS EARTH,
YOU WILL AGREE,
GETS MORE INK
THAN NAMATH'S
KNEE?

FORGIVE ME,
JOYCE KILMER.
Bill Gallo

AT HALF MAST

Anybody who was alive when John F. Kennedy was assassinated in 1963 knows what an overwhelming tragedy that was. I was at work on a cartoon about football picks when *The News'* Inquiring Photographer, John Stapleton, alerted me to the unfathomable. Like everyone else, I was stunned. I wanted to draw something special, something more than just a cartoon, something profound. I thought of JFK as our leader, our captain—regardless of whether you agreed with him—and Whitman's words came to mind. There was no need to show his face or even mention his name; the meaning at that moment couldn't be clearer.

O Captain! my Captain! rise up and hear the bells;
Rise up—for you the flag is flung—for you the
bugle trills.
For you bouquets and ribboned wreaths—for
you the shores a-crowding,
For you they call, the swaying mass, their
eager faces turning——

WALT WHITMAN

ONE TOUCH OF VENUS

I've drawn my inspirations from a range of sources. When the Yankees were faulted for having "no arms" in their bullpen in 1987, the Venus de Milo seemed a natural, and literal, translation of that criticism. I've enjoyed reading the Greek myths, and I found in the story of Sisyphus a parallel to soccer's seemingly endless struggle to gain a foothold in America.

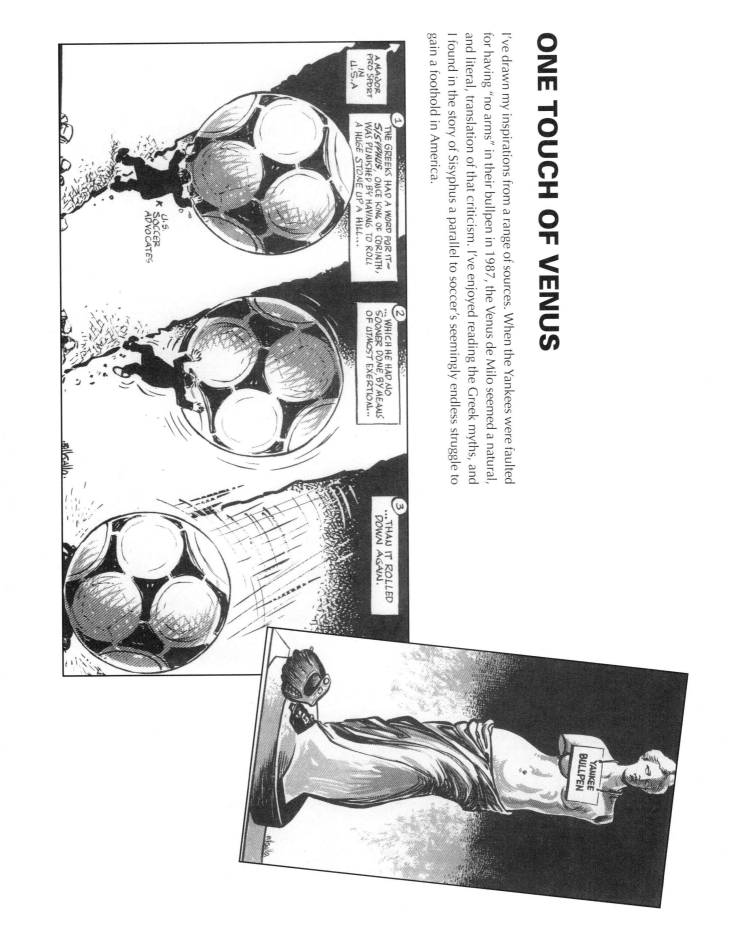

A PRINCE AMONG MEN

In 1979, Phil Simms's development into a good, steady quarterback for the Giants brought to mind the figure of Prince Valiant. I called my friend John Cullen Murphy and told the artist, "I'm going to draw your Prince Valiant." He said fine, but pointed out that the prince has black hair and Simms is blond. Again, a little dramatic license was in order. And when Joe Montana added another Super Bowl title and MVP trophy to his résumé in 1990, I likened him to everyone from Shakespeare to Snoopy (in the Louvre).

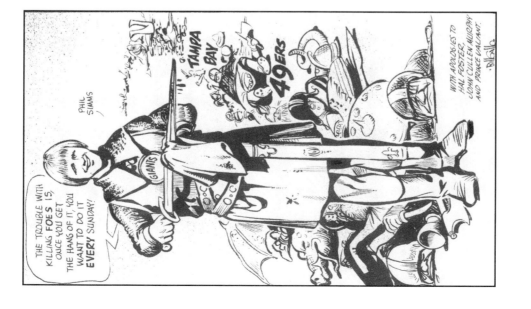

SOS

The demise of the *Titanic* is shorthand for catastrophe, and I used that image in 1981 as a baseball strike threatened to sink the season.

Two Hollywood hits, meanwhile, inspired the cartoons on the facing page: *Bonnie and Clyde* was recast with Basement Bertha and White Sox manager Eddie Stanky in 1968, and the 1997 blockbuster *Titanic* was the basis of a lighthearted comment on an unsinkable president.

INSPIRED BY THE CLASSICS

STRIKE THREE

Baseball flirted with labor disaster on more than one occasion, and a revised *Gone With the Wind* dramatized the shaky relationship between the major leagues and the fans. When a strike finally did wipe out a season, in 1994, a shadow was cast on the world of baseball—a grim image that was used on the front page of *The News*.

CHAPTER NINE

OH, NO,
IT'S A SCANDAL

HIGHS
AND LOWS

I try to be fair. I don't want to be highhanded or holier-than-thou. The worst thing is to be pedantic. Usually, I like to see how the story turns out. You don't pick on these athletes; the story picks on them. And the story came out because they were doing something.

Oh, I realize they're young, and in a lot of cases you've got to feel for them. In many instances, the damn drugs beat them. But you have to address it, as I did with these drawings. The one at the top, a takeoff on my "Two Kids Talkin' Sports," was a 1988 comment on an epidemic of high-profile drug use.

DRAWING A CROWD

FALLEN IDOL

There are a number of ways to dramatize the power of drugs to ruin lives, but it always comes back to kids, and my front-page illustration for *The News* in 1987 let it be known that Mets star Dwight Gooden had disappointed a lot of youngsters with his admission of drug abuse.

FIGHT TO THE FINISH

When former Dodgers pitcher Steve Howe attempted a comeback with the Yankees in 1991 after numerous drug suspensions, he was up against a formidable foe, and I was in his corner.

At right, I offered similar encouragement to Darryl Strawberry, a Met who was fighting a problem with the bottle in 1990.

LOSING STREAK

Yes, these stories are reported more now, but it's also gotten worse. We live in a permissive society these days. The image of the athlete has taken a beating, as I portrayed here.

ALL BETS ARE OFF

My outlook has changed as I've gotten older. I wouldn't say I've mellowed. I'd call it smarter, more patient, less of a know-it-all. I say, "Let's look at this."

My approach was by-the-book in 1963 when the Packers' star running back Paul Hornung, along with Detroit Lions lineman Alex Karras, were suspended for betting on their teams. The picture was less clear twenty-six years later when baseball banished its all-time base-hits leader, Pete Rose, also amid gambling allegations.

A THORNY QUESTION

In the case of Pete Rose, the public has not been privy to all the evidence. It's certainly hard for me to believe, though, that a competitor like Rose ever dumped a game or otherwise changed the outcome, as happened in the Black Sox scandal of 1919.

SOMEWHERE, A WRONG TURN

Tigers pitcher Denny McLain, major-league baseball's last 30-game winner (in 1968), had also faced gambling accusations—and been suspended for half a season and declared bankruptcy—when I placed him in the context of a bigger game in this 1972 drawing. He moved right around the board, rising to two-time Cy Young greatness, falling into oblivion and beyond as an incarcerated felon.

IT'S A SCANDAL

TACKLING AN ISSUE

In 1999, I came out solidly in favor of Lawrence Taylor being accepted into football's Hall of Fame. He was a legendary linebacker for the Giants, and he made his presence known in my 1986 drawing below. His substance-abuse problems off the field were irrelevant to his Hall of Fame eligibility, as far as I was concerned. Being a nice guy or not doesn't enter into it, or would Ty Cobb be in baseball's Hall of Fame?

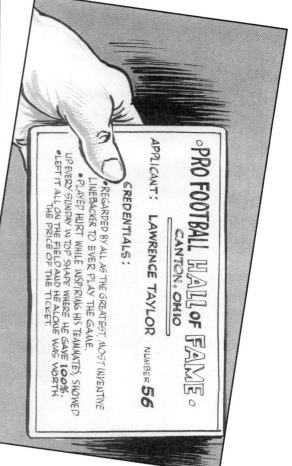

LOOKING AT THE GOOD SIDE

I don't get discouraged by all the stories of lives gone wrong, because there are so many good ones in sports. The bad ones are still not the majority. There's the star that gets into trouble, and then there are solid citizens like baseball's Cal Ripken, Jr., and hockey's Wayne Gretzky. Ripken was a tonic for baseball in 1995 when he broke Lou Gehrig's seemingly untouchable record for consecutive games played. I sent "Greatzky" my best upon his retirement in 1999.

FIRST-CLASS GUY

Don Mattingly was the epitome of a role model, a low-key guy who lived an exemplary life and worked hard at being an exceptional ballplayer. Outside of Babe Ruth, even outstanding athletes have to work at maintaining their skills.

CHAPTER TEN

A GOODBYE
TO THE GREATS

LEO O'MEALIA

It's nice to remember the fellas who are gone. There's a healthy sentimentality to it. Sure, it may be dramatic—"that big ballpark in the sky"—but it would be nice if it were true, that they're all up there, looking down from "the balcony," as I sometimes call it.

Sometimes corny works, sometimes clichés fit. You can't throw anything away. You use everything in the bag. You look at it, and if you don't like it, you put it right back in the bag. If it fits, you put it on, like an old hat.

How do you represent the memory, the lingering image of a departed subject? By breaking up the lines in the drawing with white paint, almost as if the person is fading away. A sense of distance can also be conveyed with a series of descending lines. I employed that technique in a tribute to my mentor, Leo O'Mealia, who died on May 7, 1960. His signature lion completed the sentiment.

BABE RUTH

February 6, 1895—August 16, 1948

Using the broken-line technique, I was able to place Babe Ruth right in the stands as Henry Aaron chased the Babe's career home-run mark. This drawing echoed one I had done in 1961, when the slugger's single-season mark for homers had been the target. The Babe loved kids, which gave this setting some credence.

LOU GEHRIG

June 19, 1903—June 2, 1941

Lou Gehrig faced death by counting his life's blessings in an emotional address at Yankee Stadium. I recalled that famous speech in 1964, on its twenty-fifth anniversary.

ROBERTO CLEMENTE

August 18, 1934—December 31, 1972

Roberto Clemente, the Pirates' Hall of Fame outfielder, was very serious-looking in life. He was intense. He played with a lot of finesse, glided on the field, yet he was especially focused, and I tried to convey that in my portrait done right after his death in a plane crash while on a humanitarian mission.

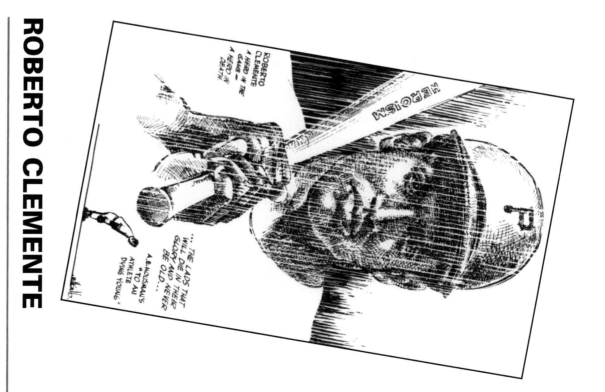

JESSE OWENS

September 12, 1913—March 31, 1980

I met Jesse Owens once in Washington and found him to be gentlemanly and articulate. He had a lot to say about the 1936 Olympics in Berlin, when his gold medals in track and the long jump punctured Hitler's master-race delusion. He spoke to me mostly about a fellow track man, Marty Glickman, who also should have run in those Olympics for the U.S. but was excluded amid the anti-Semitism of that place and time. Owens felt bad that Marty had not been allowed to run.

He also told me about his concentration during those Games. He knew that Hitler was in the stands, but he was so focused that it didn't get in his way.

Jesse enjoyed his celebrity and was upbeat. I remembered him that way upon his death in 1980.

ARTHUR ASHE

July 10, 1943—February 6, 1993

"TO BE A MAN IS TO FEEL THAT ONE'S OWN STONE CONTRIBUTES TO BUILDING THE EDIFICE OF THE WORLD."

BORROWED FROM "ANTOINE DE SAINT EXUPÉRY"

Arthur Ashe

U.S. OPEN

Arthur Ashe was someone I respected a lot. He protested racial injustice by winning on the tennis court, including the 1968 U.S. Open and at Wimbledon in 1975. My cartoon noted his contribution to the world after pneumonia claimed the AIDS-weakened champ in 1993. The occasion of this drawing was the dedication in 1997 of New York's Arthur Ashe Stadium, home to the U.S. Open and a fitting monument to a man of dignity.

JIM VALVANO

March 10, 1946—April 28, 1993

You had to admire the way college basketball coach Jim Valvano handled the cancer that ultimately killed him. The way he told everyone else to fight it: never give up, never give up. He was giving us something as he was dying. That's pretty courageous.

PAUL "BEAR" BRYANT

September 11, 1913—January 26, 1983

As noted earlier with my JFK salute, the subject need not appear in a tribute. When University of Alabama football coach Bear Bryant died, all I had to draw was his trademark hat. It was like George Burns's cigar. This hat *is* Bear Bryant.

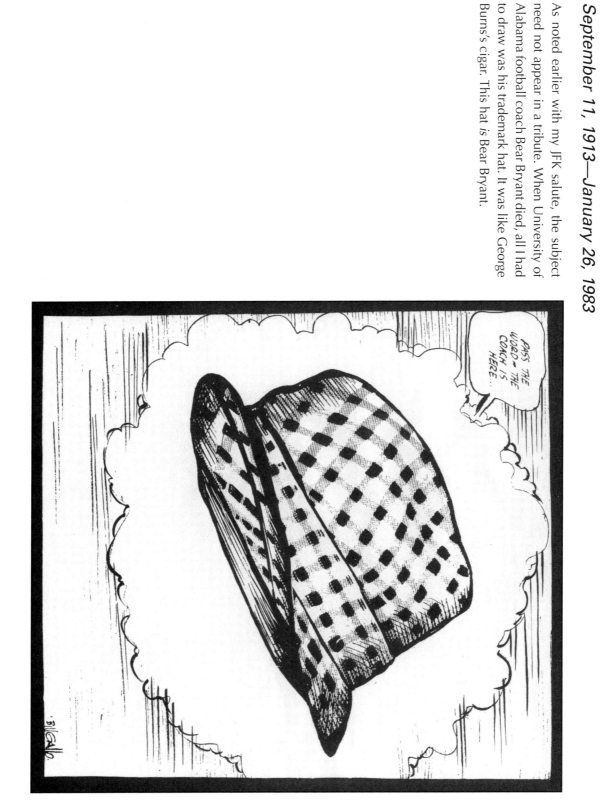

GIL HODGES

April 4, 1924—April 2, 1972

CASEY STENGEL

July 30, 1890—September 29, 1975

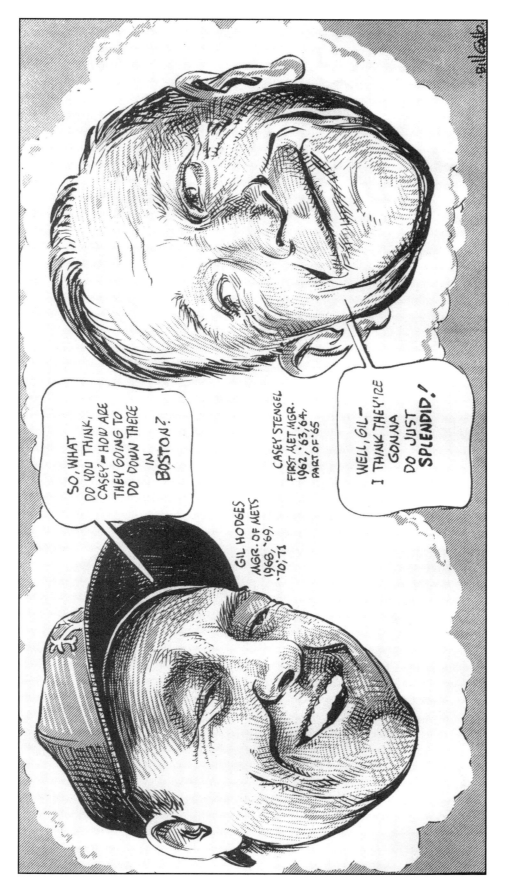

The mood needn't always be somber with these drawings, either. During the Mets' championship year in 1986, I had two of their former (and late) managers looking down in enjoyment. Casey Stengel's impish spirit seems to be rubbing off on the more reserved Gil Hodges.

A GOODBYE TO THE GREATS

PAYNE STEWART

January 30, 1957—October 25, 1999

October is the time of the baseball playoffs and New York had an exciting postseason in 1999, with both the Mets and Yankees trying to make it a Sub- way Series. Then came the news of golfer Payne Stewart's death in an airplane accident, and sud- denly even the World Series seemed insignificant.

WALTER PAYTON

July 25, 1954–November 1, 1999

Walter Payton's death from illness was not as unexpected as Stewart's but no less sorrowful.

Here's my farewell to the NFL's all-time leading rusher.

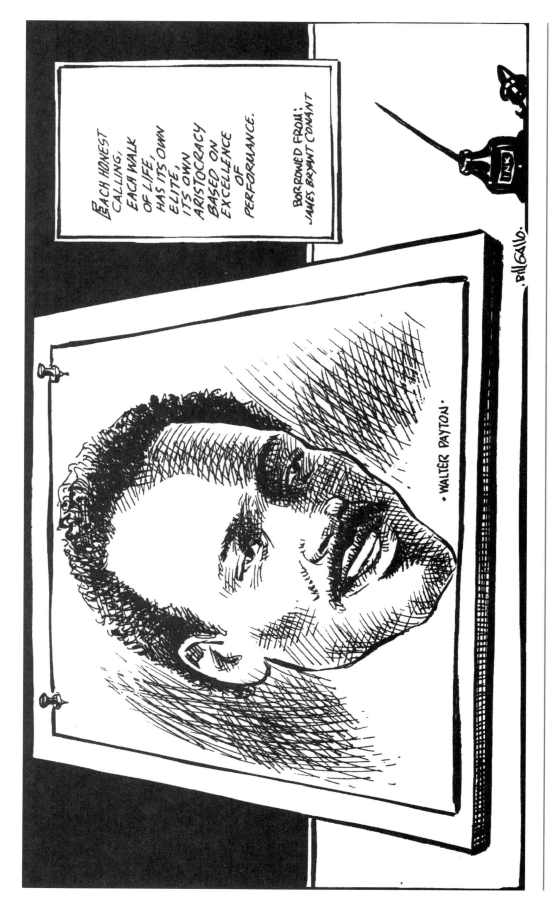

EACH HONEST CALLING, EACH WALK OF LIFE, HAS ITS OWN ELITE, ITS OWN ARISTOCRACY BASED ON EXCELLENCE OF PERFORMANCE.

BORROWED FROM: JAMES BRYANT CONANT

· WALTER PAYTON ·

BILL GALLO.

A GOODBYE TO THE GREATS

THURMAN MUNSON

June 7, 1947—August 2, 1979

The word of Thurman Munson's death in August 1979 reached me while I was delivering the sports segment of the *Daily News'* old radio show. In the middle of my spiel, *News* sports columnist Mike Lupica dashed into the studio with the report that the Yankees' catcher and captain had been killed in a plane crash. I gave this information to the listeners live, wrapped up the radio segment and got out of there, thinking: "I've got to replace my cartoon."

I had already completed the pending induction into baseball's Hall of Fame of Willie Mays and my close friend *News* columnist Dick Young. But that drawing would not see print. By the time I was in the *News* Building elevator, heading from the fifth-floor studio to the seventh-floor newsroom, I knew what I was going to draw. When something big happens, I work that way. My mind works very fast; it sharpens under pressure.

In this drawing I wanted it to look like he's gone, but still looking at the symbol of baseball, which is kids. Maybe the symbol has changed now, maybe it would be a dollar sign, but in my mind at that time it was always kids. Baseball definitely starts with kids. Kids playing in the sandlot.

Munson is watching over the kids that he left behind. That was my immediate thought, that he must be looking down, that he's away now but . . . It gets kind of corny, I guess. Maybe I think that way. It's a sentimental thing, and why not? I think I was right, because I've had so many requests for copies. Twenty years later, I still get requests for this drawing.

No Game Today—August 3, 1979

The look on Munson's face is almost saying, "Don't be sad." But the kids, they're walking the Earth, they're in the real world, so they have no heart to play. I put them in silhouette to make it more somber. Make the reality somber. The fantasy is there in the heavens saying, "Keep up the game."

CHAPTER ELEVEN

YOU'VE GOT TO BE A FOOTBALL HERO

WHEN YOU'RE A JET

Joe Namath was among those sports figures I call The Stirrers, winners who make things happen. Namath was high-profile from the time he signed with the Jets in 1965 for the then-whopping sum of $427,000. The man who brought him to New York, Sonny Werblin, was an impresario who appreciated star power. "When you see a guy bigger than life, you know it," Werblin once told me. "Namath had it."

Joe proved him right when he led the Jets, of the still-suspect American Football League, to victory in the Super Bowl in January 1969. In those days of the *Apollo* space missions, I compared that win to a lunar landing (and anticipated the Mets' championship later that year). I also painted Joe Namath and his coach, Weeb Ewbank, in their moment of triumph.

WINNER BY A NOSE

In addition to a great quarterback's arm, Joe had a great nose for a cartoon subject. I don't mean this in an insulting way. You just love the guys who have something extra in their face; it enhances the drawing. I gave Joe's nose plenty of play even as I likened his delicate knees to a Grecian urn, fragile yet valuable, in the cartoon below, from August 1974. (Charley Winner had by then taken over from his father-in-law, Ewbank, as Jets coach.) I also drew attention to Namath's chronic tardiness by assembling the other players in "whatzisname's" likeness.

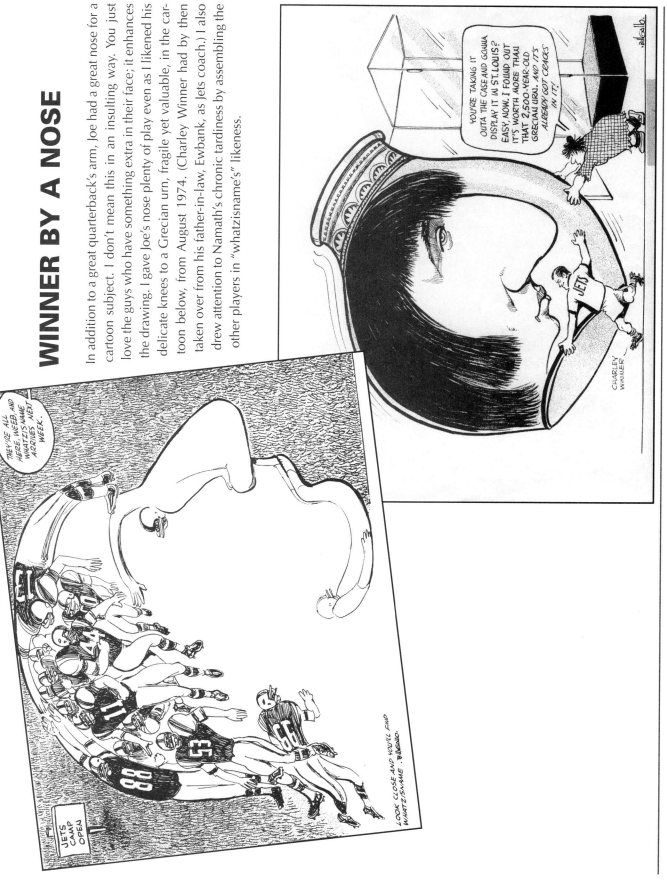

NO ORDINARY JOE

A lot of people were glad to see the flashy quarterback suit up again in November 1972 following an injury, and cartoonists were no exception. When Joe left the team for good in 1977, successor Richard Todd had to fill not only Namath's white shoes but his image, which was huge and indelible.

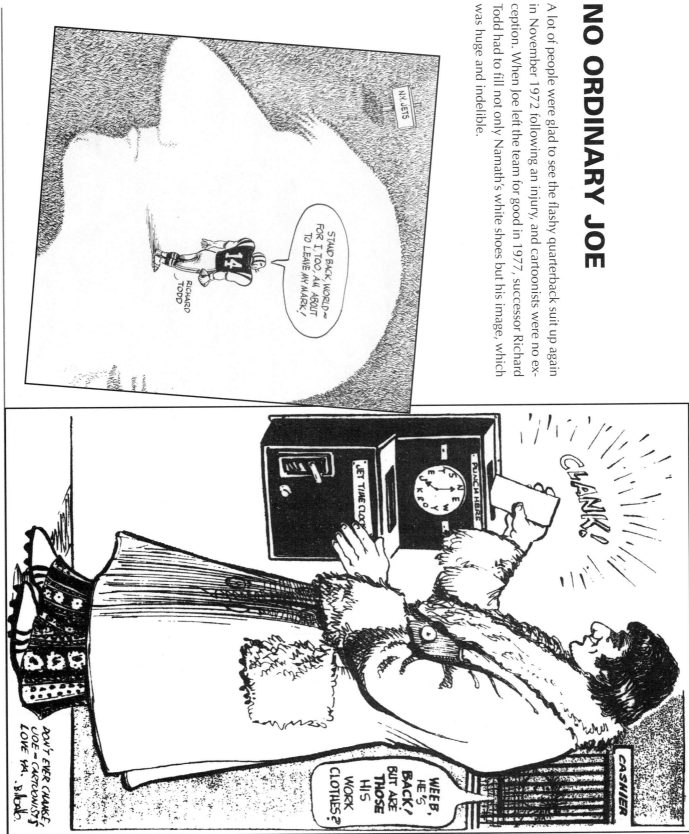

BROADWAY JOE AT THIRTY

A lot was made of Namath's womanizing and drinking, but I found this image to be driven largely by the media. "Broadway Joe" was kind of invented. Sure, Namath was a free spirit and a helluva quarterback, but the persona was more interesting than the guy himself, who seemed quiet, dedicated, and studious. He couldn't be that good yet that frivolous. After his playing days were over, he worked at being an actor (successful or not), got married, had kids—was a serious guy.

That's the side of him I conveyed in this July 1973 study of Joe, which I did in a loose, sketchy, pen-and-ink style. It accompanied a column I wrote about Namath turning thirty, the age back then for entering the Establishment. I went around interviewing football notables, asking if they thought Joe still had it. Most of them said yes and spoke highly of him, including Don Shula, the coach Namath had beaten in the Super Bowl a few years before. Giants president Wellington Mara said, "He can join my establishment any time he wants to."

YOU'VE GOT TO BE A FOOTBALL HERO

TWO OF THE BEST, NO DOUBT

Two of the greatest on the gridiron were Jim Brown and Joe Montana. They played different positions for different teams in different eras: Brown retired as a running back for the Cleveland Browns in 1966, well before Montana arrived as quarterback for the San Francisco 49ers in 1979. But they shared a terrific independence in the way they played the game. Jim Brown shared some of his views on football with me when he dropped by *The News* in January 1985.

Never did you see any sign of doubt in the play of Jim Brown or Joe Montana. You never saw them make an "aw-shucks" gesture. You knew that *they* knew exactly what they were going to do, whether it worked out or not. If it didn't work out the first time, it would the second. It usually worked out the first time, though.

In 1989, I made a quick trip to Montana country shortly before a 49ers playoff game.

YOU'VE GOT TO BE A FOOTBALL HERO

JOHNNY U

I loved watching Johnny Unitas play. People called him the ultimate gambler, but he knew exactly what he was doing with every pass he threw. When he was on his game, he was just superb—like on December 28, 1958, when he led the Baltimore Colts over the New York Giants for the NFL title in "The Greatest Game Ever Played." A few days after that landmark clash in Yankee Stadium, I conveyed my appreciation of Unitas via the drawing board.

I admired his quarterback's stance, the way he would plant his feet and stay in the pocket. A lot of nervous quarterbacks dance around, but every step Unitas took was meaningful. He saw the whole field, so he could become inventive during a play. He had a command of his team and of himself, and I seized on his leadership qualities in the cartoon at right, drawn in January 1971 before Super Bowl V. For my money, Unitas was the best quarterback of them all. He dominated the football field.

MR. ROONEY

Art Rooney, founder and longtime owner of the Pittsburgh Steelers, was a wonderful man, an old-school gentleman who was one of the real people in sports. He lived in the same Pittsburgh neighborhood all his life, was married to the same woman for fifty years, a steady guy.

He started as a boxer and was genuinely tough, which means that he knew how to handle himself and didn't bully. A phony tough guy tells you he's tough; a genuinely tough guy keeps his arsenal in reserve and doesn't have to prove anything.

He knew I wrote a boxing column, which was one of the ways we got to know one another. He also liked some cartoons I had drawn about the Steelers and asked for them. I met him at several sports functions, we exchanged letters, and he eventually became one of my favorites.

I called him "Mr. Rooney." I couldn't get myself to call him "Art," although he told me to do so. It was that old-fashioned respect. He was the only one I called "Mister."

I wished him well in this 1980 drawing as the Steelers pursued, and won, their fourth Super Bowl. Before he died in 1988, Mr. Rooney left me with two cherished gifts: autographed footballs from the Super Bowl. I would never part with them, and some day they'll be passed on to my sons.

MEN OF STEEL

Pittsburgh's "Steel Curtain" defense loomed large during their Super Bowl run from 1975 to 1980, and quarterback Roger Staubach of the Dallas Cowboys had to face it in two of those Bowl battles. Before the Steelers' 1980 Super Bowl match against the Rams, I made use of a popular soda commercial that showed Pittsburgh's "Mean" Joe Greene giving his game jersey to a young fan.

STANDING TALL

Heroism comes in many forms. In the case of Mike Utley, a former lineman for the Detroit Lions, it meant simply taking a few steps. Utley was paralyzed in a game against the Rams in November 1991; after years of struggle and with the support of braces and a friend on each side, he finally was able to walk a few yards in February 1999. I don't know Utley, but I *had* to do this cartoon. I wanted to bring out this guy's courage. I was utterly impressed when I watched him take those steps, to learn that it was the first time he had done it in more than seven years.

Those steps did something for people, for those disabled people who might say they can't do it. He says, "I can." Some may think that's hokey, but I think that's *real*.

TODAY WE'LL NOT DEAL WITH WINS AND LOSSES IN ARENAS ~ INSTEAD WE GO TO ANOTHER BATTLEFIELD ~ THE FIELD OF COURAGE AND DESIRE...

...THIS IS ABOUT **MIKE UTLEY**, FORMER DETROIT LION OFFENSIVE LINEMAN, WALKING A FEW STEPS. IT WAS AKIN TO CLIMBING MOUNT EVEREST. THESE WERE HIS FIRST STEPS IN SEVEN YEARS.

IT WAS HEARTENING TO SEE AND I THOUGHT OF THIS LINE BY CERVANTES WRITTEN MANY YEARS AGO: "THE GUTS CARRY THE FEET, NOT THE FEET THE GUTS."

* ONE MAN WITH COURAGE MAKES A MAJORITY.

ANDREW JACKSON

BILL GALLO

THE KID CAN PLAY

Children at play are always grist for my mill, and I have found such subjects within my own family. Here, the running back named Henry was modeled after my nephew. This October 1963 drawing followed a big clash between the Giants and the Browns.

DRAWING A CROWD

ARMCHAIR QUARTERBACK

Like many sports fans, I've watched a lot of football on television, as is documented in this cartoon from the 1960s (costarring my wife, Dolores, in an off-panel role).

I use my piggie system, based on the movie star ratings, to grade the Super Bowl. This is from the January 1999 match between the Denver Broncos and the Atlanta Falcons.

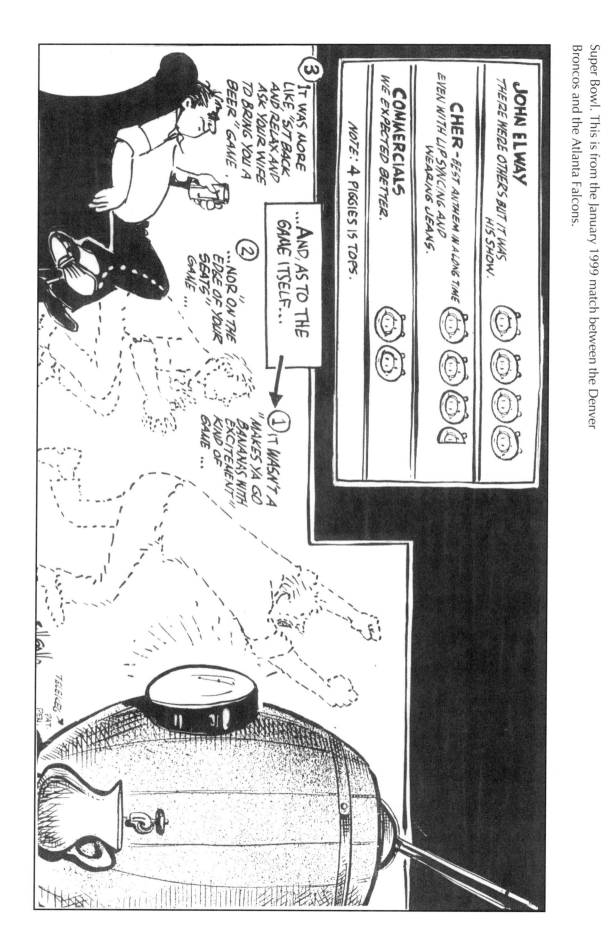

CHAPTER TWELVE

IWO JIMA
AND VIETNAM

OFF TO WAR

Once you're in combat, it's such a shocking reality. It's no longer a game. You want it over with, you want out. You want the war to end. Once you see combat, the John Wayne-ism is gone. All that "Over the top, fellas" and other b.s.? I never heard anybody say that. "Get your ass down!"—that was more the cliché.

You get old fast. You're twenty-one, and in a sense you're old. You know about your mortality. You know that it could be you the next day. At first, you say, "It's not going to be me." Then you wake up in the morning and a couple of guys are gone, and you say, "That was close." After a while, you realize, "Yes, it could be me."

SELF PORTRAIT
OF A
20-YEAR-OLD
MARINE
JUST OUT
OF BOOT
CAMP
1943

In 1969, during the Vietnam War, I traveled to the Far East as part of a USO tour. Flying across the Pacific, I passed over a dark, desolate island that looked like a hatchet. It was Iwo Jima.

It was the eeriest of feelings looking down on the place where I had landed many years before with the Fourth Marine Division. The names of those with me then were like any others from any neighborhood: Ozzie, the affable guy from Brooklyn; Eddie Killian out of Detroit; Joe Bruni and Stan Lacey from New York; and Elmer Grant Murphy, a big guy with a big Southern drawl from Huntington, West Virginia. I remember them all well. You don't forget people you lived with through a war.

And I remember Popernack, Corporal George Popernack, the man left aboard ship while the rest of us clambered over the side, climbed down rope ladders and got into the Higgins boats that would take us to the island's black shores. I remember how, all those years ago, Popernack died on Iwo.

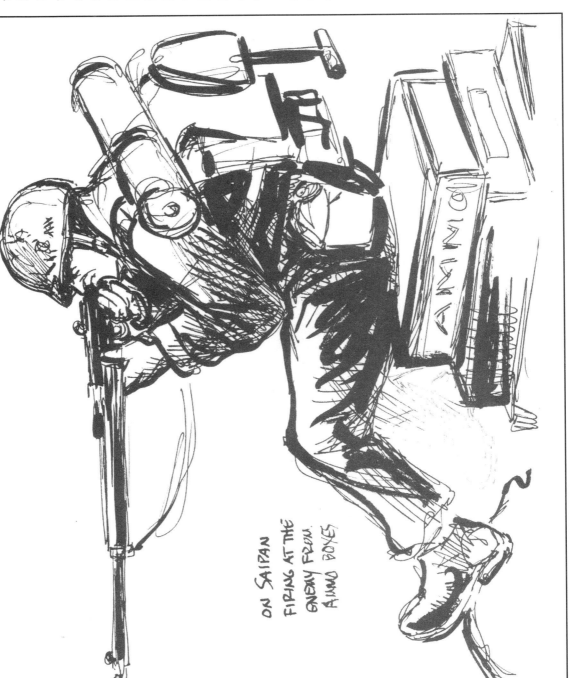

ON SAIPAN
FIRING AT THE
ENEMY FROM
AMMO BOXES

THE NEED TO TAKE IWO

We had to capture this Godforsaken place, only 758 miles from Tokyo and 3,791 miles from Pearl Harbor. Our country desperately needed this speck of dreariness, some seven and one-half square miles, as a fighter base from which escort planes could join our B-29s on their way to bomb Japan.

It wasn't going to be easy. We had learned the hard way how formidable the enemy was on their tightly held islands. We had seen the tenacity of the Japanese in the landings of Roi-Namur, part of the Kwajalein atoll, and in the battles of Saipan and Tinian in the Marianas island chain. The optimists were saying it wouldn't be as bad as Saipan, where we had 5,981 casualties. They were wrong: Iwo Jima left us crippled, with 9,098 casualties in a division of 19,000.

COMPAT - SAIPAN
- GALO -

CORPSMAN! CORPSMAN! OVER HERE!

DEATH IN A FLASH

We landed on that ugly, almost treeless lump of volcanic ash in February 1945 and did not leave until the island was secured in late March. That is, the lucky ones left.

Fighting on Iwo was inch by inch. The entire island was the front line. The enemy had clobbered the beach with mortar fire for about two weeks. It was dark when the enemy began their mortar fire again. That afternoon, Popernack landed on the beach, days after the rest of us. We kidded him, called him Bob Hope because he came in so many days later. That night, he died.

A small group of us in a demolitions team had hoped the Japanese mortar positions could somehow be located so they might be quieted with twenty-pound satchel charges. The enemy surprised us in this campaign with a perfect pattern of mortar blasts. They were launched from well behind the enemy's lines, aimed at our installations on the beach and at one of the airfields.

As one of the big ones landed, all of us from the demolitions team plus Popernack jumped into one of the craters. Popernack took it all. By some miracle, the rest of us, our ears ringing from the blast, discovered that we had only small scratches from the sand kicking up. Pop, as we called him, never knew what hit him.

DAMAGED TANK

PROBING FOR LAND MINES ON IWO UNDER FIRE

FLAG-RAISING AND A SALUTE

Even after Iwo was called "ours," 6,820 Marines from three divisions died. An estimated 22,000 Japanese had been killed by the three divisions, 8,982 having been counted in the Fourth Division's zone alone. A thousand more were believed sealed in caves or buried by the enemy. Only forty-four prisoners were taken by our division.

One of our fallen comrades, Sergeant John Basilone of Raritan, New Jersey, had won the Medal of Honor for his gallantry in Guadalcanal. John had elected to give up Stateside duty for "just one more landing," and died on the day of landing at the foot of Mount Suribachi. His last words were reported to be, "Come on, you guys, we gotta get these guns off the beach."

I remember, like it was yesterday, the friends who fell on those black sands and were buried under it. On the fiftieth anniversary of that invasion, in February 1995, I quietly saluted the survivors and lifted a glass to all the men who never had the opportunity to be husbands and fathers and grandfathers. Guys like John Basilone and George Popernack.

IWO JIMA
· FEB. 19, 1945 ·
50 YEARS

FROM THE FOURTH MARINE DIVISION BOOK—FIRST EDITION—DEC. 1046

"OUR TANKS AND BULLDOZERS AND TRUCKS WERE SUPPORTED BY THE IRON HEARTS OF THE MEN WHO FELL IN THE SAND WHERE THEY FOUGHT... THERE WAS ONE CONSTANT REMINDER OF THIS, THE ROW AFTER ROW OF GLISTENING WHITE CROSSES AND SLABS THAT MARKED A TINY PART OF IWO BELONGING TO THE DEAD. IT SEEMED AS IF THEY HAD AGREED TO OCCUPY THIS BLACK AND WINDSWEPT BIT OF BEACH SO THAT MEN'S HOMES AND COUNTRY, THEIR IDEALS, THEIR HOPES AND ASPIRATIONS AS AMERICANS, MIGHT BE SHARED BY THE LIVING."

-BILLGALLO ©
1994

VIETNAM: ONE MAN'S JOURNEY

I went on that USO trip in 1969 believing in what the government was saying about the Vietnam War, how we had to be there to stop Communist aggression. Since I had been in the Marines Corps myself, I was a little gung-ho about it. I believed that the Marines and other soldiers in Vietnam were there willingly and favorably. But they weren't, as I found out during my twenty-eight days overseas.

I toured hospitals all over the Far East, visiting with about three hundred wounded kids, sketching them while we talked. There were plenty of amputees, some multiple amputees, because Vietnam was a war of land mines and booby traps. I sent a letter home to News editor Floyd Barger relating my observations:

When you sketch these kids, naturally you must look in their eyes—old eyes on a nineteen-year-old kid. Many times you're looking at amputees. And sometimes your legs start to go and you have to steel yourself. There are times you know you are going to get sick, and many times you want to cry. There was one kid from New York . . . I couldn't sketch him because his head was shaved and there were four incisions. We talked a bit, but he only had half his senses. . . . He remembered his name, but couldn't think where he was from. It's in cases like these that I said to myself, "What the hell am I doing here? What the hell is anybody doing here?"

I found that those kids in Vietnam were in such limbo. They didn't know who they were fighting. I realized that this was a bastard war, one without rhyme or reason, and our boys did not belong there (which would be borne out years later). I saw then that Muhammad Ali was right in his opposition to the war; it was the government that was wrong, guys like General William Westmoreland and LBJ, the president whose main concern seemed to have been not to lose a war on his watch. And by the way, what does Robert McNamara say today?

In those days, *The News* backed the war effort, as I did. But I viewed Vietnam differently when I came back. I told my wife that I would do everything in my power to keep our two sons out of this futile war. (Luckily, they were not called.) There comes a time when you have to evaluate what you've seen, and what I had just seen was the cruelest thing that could be done to America's youth.

A COMBAT VETERAN IN THE VIETNAM WAR

YOUNG, INNOCENT, BRAVE AND BEWILDERED

War stays with you, in one way or another, all your life. Sometimes it stretches into your kid's life, too.

It was a week before the holidays, and my son Bill was the plaintiff in a civil court case. He had just completed his testimony in a courtroom in West Chester, Pennsylvania, when the court clerk, a roundish and aging man, approached him and introduced himself.

"This is a long shot, Mr. Gallo," the man began, "but by any chance do you have a father—or a grandfather—who was once in the Fourth Marine Division during World War II?"

"My father was in the Marines," replied Bill.

"And is he a newspaperman in New York?" the clerk continued.

"Yes, for the *Daily News*."

Joe Leicht, the court clerk, smiled and said, "Your father and I were in combat together, even in the same foxhole on one occasion."

Leicht then told my son a few war stories—how we landed on the islands of Roi-Namur in the Marshall Islands and how we shared that foxhole during a Japanese banzai attack on Saipan and about the agonies endured on Iwo Jima.

These were accounts my son had never heard because I was never much for war stories, especially as the decades passed. But if I search my memory, I can recall that night on Saipan vividly.

That particular day, we had a rare mail call. They had dropped mail sacks over Saipan hoping to boost the morale of the guys engaged in combat. To my surprise, I was one of the guys to receive a letter. It was from a girl, and it turned out to be a Dear John letter, which basically meant goodbye.

I liked this girl a lot, but there I was facing the enemy, so I tossed the missive away and said, "What the hell." There went my girlfriend forever, I thought. I guess I must have mentioned this to my foxhole partner just before the Japanese attacked our lines.

We made it through the night and fought in the morning. Leicht and I were two lucky Marines.

Now, lo these many years later, Leicht had one more thing to tell my son in that Pennsylvania courtroom: "I can still remember your father talking a lot about a girl named Dolores. Wonder what happened to her."

Bill said, grinning:

"That's my mother."

CHAPTER THIRTEEN

GOT THE HORSE RIGHT HERE

FROM THE HORSE'S MOUTH

Racehorses aren't the most expressive of athletes. Still, there are ways to give them personality in a sports cartoon. Anything that's in a contest, that fights hard, you treat with the elements of a human. Man o' War was similar to Jack Dempsey, tough and rugged. The horse was virtually unbeatable, upset only once—by a horse fittingly named Upset. Secretariat was like an elitist, particularly when he won the Belmont by 31 lengths in 1973. That spring, I relied on plain horse sense to conclude that Secretariat would give racing its first Triple Crown winner in twenty-five years.

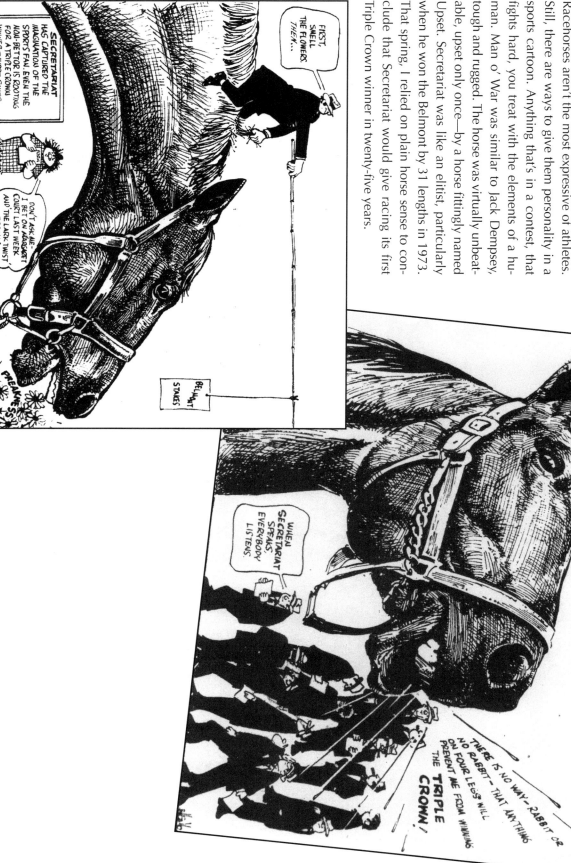

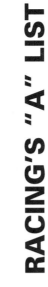

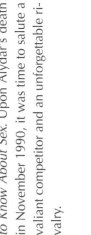

RACING'S "A" LIST

The greatest horse in my book was Affirmed because of the three terrific battles he waged with Alydar in 1978. Now if you're a bettor, you don't care if your horse wins by 31 lengths or by a nose—as Affirmed did to take the Belmont—you just want it to win. But outside of that world, the contest is the thing. It always is in sports.

No matter how hard No. 2, Alydar, tried, he couldn't quite catch Affirmed in their Triple Crown duels. When Affirmed was retired to stud in 1979, I found a new use for the book *Everything You Always Wanted to Know About Sex.* Upon Alydar's death in November 1990, it was time to salute a valiant competitor and an unforgettable rivalry.

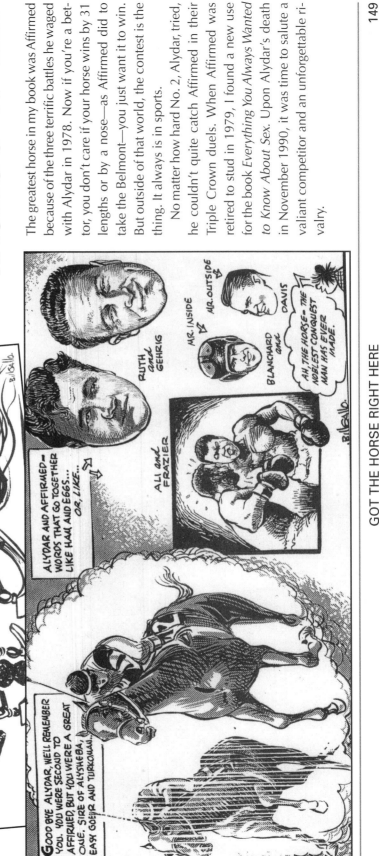

A BREED APART

In 1986, I combined the eleven Triple Crown winners into a collage of champions. Snow Chief failed to join their ranks, although he did capture the Preakness.

REIN-ING CHAMPS

The jockey also adds personality to a drawing, especially winning ones such as Eddie Arcaro, Willie Shoemaker and Steve Cauthen. I noted the change in racing royalty when Arcaro retired in 1962, and showed the young phenom Cauthen riding high in 1978.

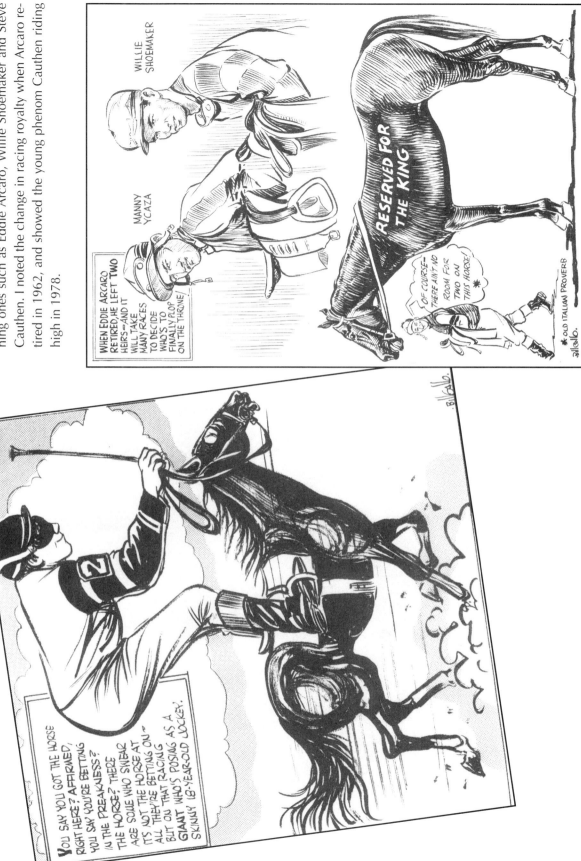

A STABLE UPBRINGING

When I go to the track, I bet the jockey. I figure if he's a good jockey, they'll treat him to a good horse. By the time of this drawing in May 1989, top jockeys had an inside track in sport's big-payday sweepstakes.

LEAP OF LOGIC

Some people like picking the long shots; I even created my character Johnny Unda as the guy who always goes for the underdog. But the behavior of the lemming was the only way to explain bettors who passed up both Affirmed and Alydar in the 1978 Derby.

DRAWING A CROWD

IN THEIR ELEMENT

I've kidded bettors by showing them so eager for action that they'll wager on police horses or brave a snowstorm to get to the track. Still, handicappers are a congenial type. They like the races and the surroundings of the track. The guy who's really hooked, who's sick on gambling, can stay home and use the phone to make bets.

THE BETTING LINE

The two-dollar bettor is my kind of guy. You go to the track to enjoy the day and see if you can break even. Like a wag once said, "I hope I break even 'cause I need the money."

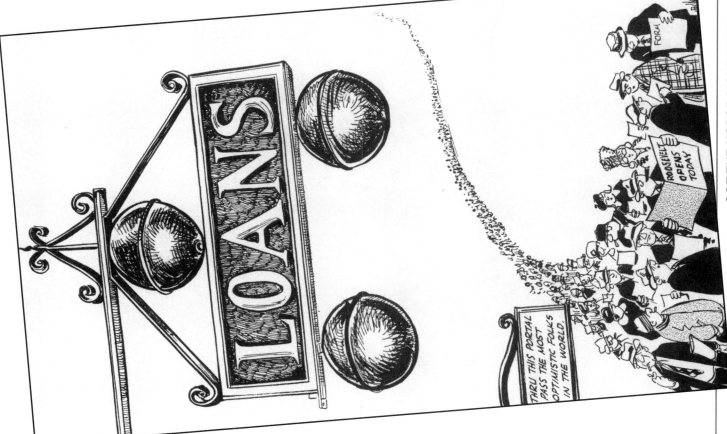

GOT THE HORSE RIGHT HERE

IT TAKES A THIEF

On November 12, 1969, three men robbed an armored car of $1.3 million—two days' receipts from New York's Aqueduct Racetrack—while the cash was en route from Queens to Manhattan. When I heard where the loot had been stolen from, an idea for a cartoon sprung to mind: a long-frustrated bettor had finally settled the score. My drawing "A Day at the Races" ran on November 14, "Dedicated to all two-dollar bettors." It was a big hit, like the Munson memorial drawing. The funniest and the saddest of cartoons have gotten the most play.

Yes, I did catch some flak from people who said I was promoting theft. But thirty years later I still get requests for this drawing. It was so popular that I heard that the famed bank robber Willie Sutton wanted it. I gave it to a News police reporter to pass along to Sutton, and as far as I know, "A Day at the Races" made it to Willie.

CHAPTER FOURTEEN

FAIR BALL

PAR FOR THE COURSE

The first time I became personally aware of racism—when I actually saw it in action—I had just finished Marine boot camp and was on liberty in Jacksonville, Florida. I was walking with this fella from the South, when he suddenly turned to me and said, "Come on, we have to cross the street." I asked him why. He replied, "Here's a . . . [I don't even want to use the word, the N word] . . . coming up." I said, "What the hell are you talking about? I had heard about this kind of prejudice, but seeing it astonished me.

He tugged me to go. I said, "No, are you crazy?" He went, but I didn't. I just thought, "These people are serious about this stuff."

There's subtler ways to inflict prejudice, like when a country club screens out aspiring members based on their ethnicity. I've seen how that works, too. In this cartoon, I took aim at such forms of exclusion.

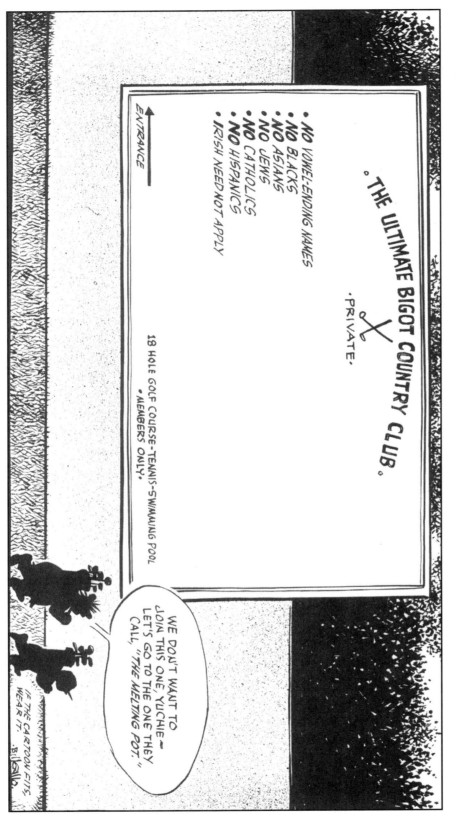

MEETING GROUND

When I was a kid in Astoria, I was teased about my Spanish heritage. At first I fought it, but then I learned to laugh at it. It became a joke when I realized it was coming from people like me. Everybody has to overcome something. I'd find that the Irish kids who were making fun of me had fathers who had been picked on. Spanish kids would be made fun of, Italian kids, black kids, Jewish kids, Greek kids. When you grow up in that neighborhood, you are not prejudiced, because everyone's in the same boat. Once you understand that, it melts all that stuff down. Kind of like what happens in these two vintage drawings of city kids.

I consider myself lucky in that I grew up where there was an ample amount of everything, a melting pot. I wasn't poisoned with prejudice.

KNOCKING ON THE DOOR

Later in life it bothered me that I had accepted the status quo of the big leagues being all white. I didn't think of it at the time—but I should have. When the impact hits, you almost want to throw away all the old records you studied years ago, about Babe Ruth and all of the rest, because so many great ballplayers were eliminated. The greatest boxers I saw were black, and they were fighting at a time when they were barred from baseball. If Joe Louis had been great at baseball, he wouldn't have been able to play against white ballplayers. That's ridiculous. It's criminal.

The public kept hearing about how great Satchel Paige was and Josh Gibson was, kept going to the Negro Leagues games to see them play. So why didn't someone say: What the hell are you doing there? Why don't you come on into the majors?

WHEN COOPERSTOWN PAIGED SATCHEL

In 1971 baseball's Hall of Fame opened its doors to the stars of the Negro Leagues, and the first such inductee, selected soon after, was Satchel Paige. Unlike Josh Gibson, Paige played long enough to finally be allowed into the majors—a forty-two-year-old "rookie" for the Cleveland Indians in 1948. He pitched into the early 1950s, then returned to toss three innings in 1965 at the age of fifty-nine.

"I never did feel any bitterness toward baseball," Satch once said. "I knew the first black man in the major leagues had to have a college education. I really believe in my soul that they got the right man when they got Jackie." He means Robinson, of course.

FAIR BALL

ALL THERE IN BLACK AND WHITE

No matter what Jackie Robinson did on the base-ball field, it was a challenge: he challenged the ball; he challenged the pitcher; he challenged the second baseman trying to put him out; he challenged Yogi Berra trying to tag him out at home plate. Talk about a guy who played to beat you. He could beat you every which way.

I had a lot of admiration for Jackie Robinson, like everybody else, because he did all these things under adverse conditions. All those slurs. I heard a few of them myself. My drawing titled "The First," with its one black face in a sea of white ones, recalled the imbalance of Jackie's breakthrough season of 1947.

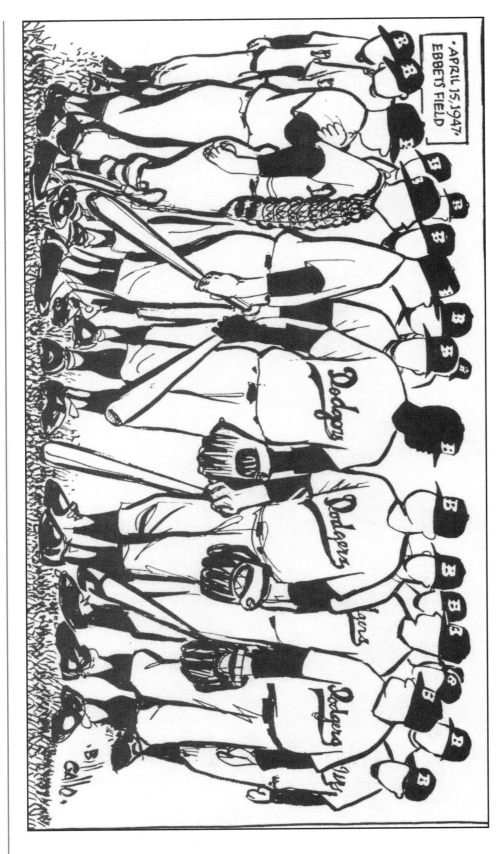

· APRIL 15, 1947 ·
EBBET'S FIELD

FAIR BALL

THANK GOD FOR JACKIE ROBINSON

I got to know Jackie when he became a New York boxing commissioner and I was covering boxing. At that point, he had a bad case of diabetes and a heart problem, but he never complained. He just was a solemn white-haired man.

We talked, but it always came back to boxing. He didn't seem to want to talk much about baseball or the Dodgers. It was like it had passed him by. There was no pep in him, no fight. And it was strange to see no fight in Jackie Robinson, the man I watched tearing up the base paths, running so hard he almost dug a trench.

Jackie died in October 1972, and in the drawing at right I recalled what that daring trailblazer had accomplished.

It was Branch Rickey who put Jackie Robinson in a Brooklyn uniform and gave the next generation of baseball fans a lot more stars to look up to. In the cartoon at left on the facing page, I paid tribute to Rickey upon his death in December 1965.

When another Robinson, Frank, became the first black manager in the major leagues in 1975, I recalled who had made it possible. That reminds me of what Dodger pitcher Joe Black once said: "When I look at my house . . . I say, 'Thank God for Jackie Robinson.'"

APRIL 15, 1947
EBBETS FIELD
BROOKLYN vs. BOSTON
AND JACKIE ROBINSON
IS IN THE LINEUP.

THANK YOU, JACKIE ROBINSON.

ME TOO.

IN THE THROWS OF CHANGE

In sports, as elsewhere, discrimination was not limited to race. I have to admit that in my generation we were kind of male chauvinists. But, little by little, women have shown they can excel in sports, too—so why would you want to be mired in that old b.s.? You have to go with the times; you can't be stuck in the mud. That's progress.

In this cartoon, with a single sentence I was able to trace the progress made over a period of eighty years. By the time the U.S. won the women's World Cup soccer tournament in July 1999, the phrase "You throw like a girl!" had been thrown out as an insult.

KING OF PROMOTION

One of the more celebrated skirmishes in the women's movement, the September 1973 tennis match between Billie Jean King and Bobby Riggs in the Astrodome was basically a testimony to Riggs's promotional skills. I believe he knew he was going to lose. Although he acted like a chauvinist, I don't think he really was one—but it helped at the gate. It got Billie Jean's dander up, which I think was a little exaggerated, too. The match wound up being good for everybody concerned, particularly King, who made $100,000 from her victory. It advanced the image of the woman athlete, and that was also a plus. Finally, it gave a cartoonist an opportunity to have some fun.

HORSING AROUND

I was called a male chauvinist myself for this cartoon, which ran in March 1969 after trailblazing jockey Barbara Jo Rubin, then age nineteen, debuted at Aqueduct Racetrack. Despite what my critics said then, I'm no chauvinist. There have been lots of women in my life—I'm a grandfather to four girls—and I've rooted for them all.

AIRING DIFFERENCES

I was again chided, though more kindly, in 1981, when I drew a cartoon celebrating the release of the hostages from Iran. The illustration at left was titled "52 Guys Talkin' Sports."

Shortly thereafter, Beth Fallon, a colleague of mine at *The News*, noted in a column that two of the fifty-two hostages were women. "I felt I had to say it not for 'our' side, the female side, but for our side—the American side," she wrote. The tone was warmhearted throughout, and I had Bertha respond in kind.

SMASHING PERFORMANCES

Tennis great Chris Evert has been a favorite of mine since July 1972, when she reached the semifinals at Wimbledon as a spunky seventeen-year-old. In the cartoon below, I welcomed that achievement.

A seven-time French Open winner, Evert was terrific on the clay courts, as Bertha notes at left.

TENNIS ROYALTY

Billie Jean King ruled the tennis world herself during the 1960s and 1970s. This regal portrait of her came after she took the Wimbledon crown in 1972.

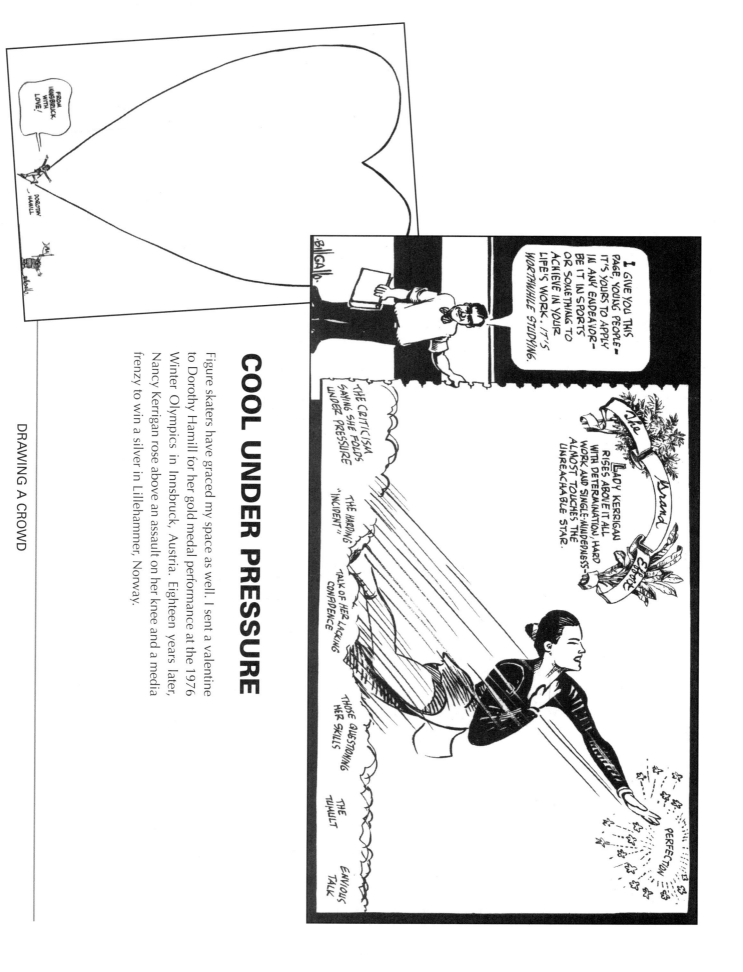

COOL UNDER PRESSURE

Figure skaters have graced my space as well. I sent a valentine to Dorothy Hamill for her gold medal performance at the 1976 Winter Olympics in Innsbruck, Austria. Eighteen years later, Nancy Kerrigan rose above an assault on her knee and a media frenzy to win a silver in Lillehammer, Norway.

THE LADY IS A CHAMP

In the 1998 Winter Olympics, the U.S. embraced its gold-medal women's hockey team, then got an additional kick from the aforementioned soccer squad the following year. About this time, I invoked the spirit of a remarkable athlete, Babe Didrikson Zaharias, in the cartoon that appears on the following page. There was a lot of controversy surrounding Zaharias—people saying she wasn't a feminine lady—but this admirable woman took it with a grain of salt and helped open things up for generations to come.

CHAPTER FIFTEEN

THE CASE FOR CASEY

YOU CAN LOOK IT UP

If you listened to him, Casey Stengel made a lot of sense, believe it or not. Stengel was great company off the field. We newspapermen used to sit with him in Mama Leone's restaurant until the wee hours. He'd do all the talking, telling amusing stories and helping out the writers to boot. He'd say, "I've got a story for you, kid. Take it down." True or false, it was a good story.

He would never use names when talking about someone. It was always "that fella in center field" or "the big guy," "the skinny guy," "the guy with the bandy legs." He used to call me "The Artist."

The Artist would tell people he could draw Casey's face with just eight lines. I also drew his face using the years of all his world championships, a cartoon that hung in his California home. This illustration dates to 1960, when the seventy-year-old Stengel was let go by the Yanks. It was sad, but the only one who wasn't sad about it was Casey himself. He seemed to know what it was all about. He didn't like it, he wanted to call his own shots, but he wasn't the kind of guy who was going to quit.

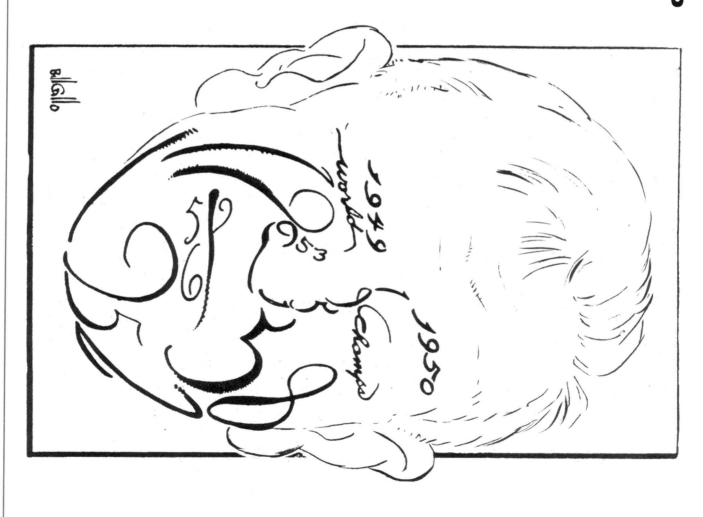

I'D GROWN ACCUSTOMED TO HIS FACE

When the Yankees replaced Stengel with Ralph Houk, it created a void on my drawing board. Then the expansion Mets hired Casey as their first manager, and I celebrated the return of that marvelous mug to my *News* cartoons.

Casey was reunited with his old Yankees general manager, George Weiss, but on the talent-starved Mets, Stengel was hired strictly for his marketing magic. They needed to put people in the stands, and Casey was a great salesman. He and Muhammad Ali were the greatest sports salesmen—the best at promotion—that I ever saw.

Like Ali, Stengel was the real deal. He may have been an actor, but he was no phony. I knew when Casey was putting people on. It was like you were in a select club if he picked on you. He'd tease you about your clothes, say something like, "Where'd you get that—Sears and Roebuck?" If he didn't like you, he just wouldn't bother with you. He'd give them a "Yup" or a "Nope."

CASEY AT THE BAT RACK

While the world laughed at him, Casey, in reality, was laughing at us. That impish spirit was on view in a cartoon from July 1965, when he was fined $200 by National League president Warren Giles for smoking in the dugout. Another drawing, from the heyday of the Beatles, showed the master marketer at work.

WIT AND WISDOM

The Mets nearly threw a monkey wrench into the Cardinals' pennant drive at the end of the 1964 season, much to Casey's delight. His managing days with the Mets were long over when, in 1969, Bertha sought him out to help understand life's great mysteries. That was only right, since Casey was partly responsible for Bertha's creation.

THE CASE FOR CASEY

CASEY'S KID

People might argue that Stengel won because of all the great players he had—DiMaggio, Mantle, Ford, etc.—but when you make it to ten World Series and win seven of them, it's more than luck. Besides, Casey was highly criticized when he used the platoon system to match right-handed batters against left-handed pitchers (and vice versa)—and that turned out to be a stroke of genius.

When Billy Martin led the Yankees to a World Series victory in the late '70s, I visualized Casey in the heavens smiling down on his "adopted kid." He loved Martin's type of managing.

TALKING A GOOD GAME

In the summer of 1972, I visited Casey in retirement in Glendale, California. What was to have been a half-hour stop turned into a five-hour seminar by "The Perfesser," delivered in that meandering language known as Stengelese. The question that started it all was: Do you think the Yankees can win the pennant?

Answered Casey: "They have an easy way of discharging you but they always do it at the wrong time—they lost Berra and they won a pennant with him. Right now, I'm working for the Mets. I thought they were going to do it, but nobody can satisfy you at third base unless it be now with [Jim] Fregosi. But catching is the best part of the ballclub.

"The Yankees? They're experienced people. Houk knows his stuff. When I had DiMaggio out there, he played crippled better than anybody, and in 1960 I pitched Ford and they haven't scored off him yet.

"They gave [Elston] Howard a chance, an excellent catcher, but he had to wait for Berra—he had to live in New York without disturbing anybody.

"Berra and myself look the same in a uniform. I always had my hand in my pocket and his clothes didn't hang on him too good—you couldn't tell us apart."

I again asked about the Yanks' chances. . . .

THE CASE FOR CASEY

"Well, did you remember DiMaggio ever diving for a ball? Never. He had an uncanny start—it looked like he could go after a ball at the sound of an echo."

I tried to steer him back to the Yankees' place in the pennant race.

"I like three of his players, but they haven't done enough for me yet. I think the bunting situation is terrible. Nobody can bunt anymore, or they say they can't. It's as easy as chopping wood. Why I have a man in Australia learning how to bunt.

"Let me tell you, though, some of the most brilliant men in baseball are scouts. Listen, I get a thousand a month just sittin' here. I don't have to watch them anymore.

"And one more thing, if Ted Williams could see the ball so good up at the plate, why don't umpires stand sideways to call balls and strikes?"

And so it went. It was our last visit together, for Casey died a few years later. Here's a drawing that takes us one more time around the diamond with a man who was a real gem.

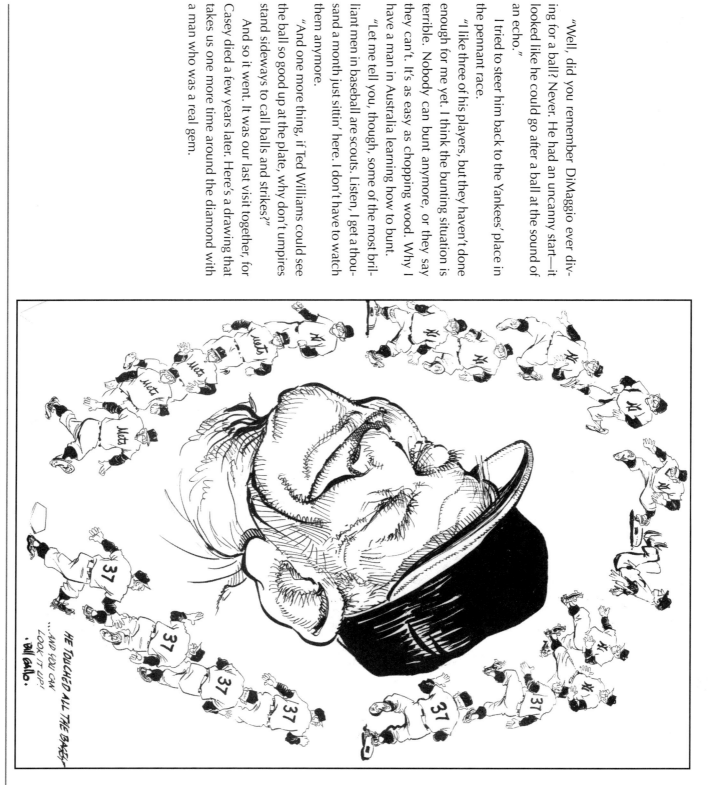

HE TOUCHED ALL THE BASES—
...AND YOU CAN
LOOK IT UP!
· Bill Gallo ·

CHAPTER SIXTEEN

MONEY TALKS

PISTOL
PETE
MARAVICH

$1 MILLION SALARY

THE SIX-FIGURE-SALARY MAN

You don't see colorful characters like Casey Stengel among today's managers and coaches. Maybe that's what money does. When money becomes the overriding thing, there's not much room for levity.

I've drawn attention to star contracts from the days when $100,000 a year was the height of affluence in baseball. That was the figure Mickey Mantle agreed to in 1964 when "the AL's only six-figure-salary man," as *The News* described him, hit it big for the second straight season. The following year, I figured that Notre Dame's Heisman-winning quarterback John Huarte could travel in style after the Jets paid him $200,000 to be Joe Namath's backup.

REELING IN A CATFISH

One of the first to strike it rich as a free agent was Jim (Catfish) Hunter. Freed by an arbiter from his contract with the Oakland A's, the twenty-eight-year-old Cy Young winner was on just about every team's Christmas shopping list in 1974, as depicted in my holiday greeting for that year. In a sign of things to come, George Steinbrenner would land him for the Yankees.

SALES PITCHES

The situation was replayed in December 1981, when Reggie Jackson was up for grabs. Atlanta owner Ted Turner looked to be Santa this time, but the Angels would end up with the big present. And when Don Sutton pulled down millions from the Houston Astros, I began to wonder what the likes of Ford, Gibson and Koufax would be making. Note Bertha's reference to my old admirer Willie Sutton, who once said he robbed banks because "that's where the money is."

IT'S ALL IN THE GAME

Athletes from other sports were getting the opportunity to cash in, too, including basketball star Pete Maravich and quarterback Joe Namath.

As the salaries started climbing, I redefined the old "Who's on First" routine made famous by Abbott and Costello.

MONEY TALKS

CASH AND CARRY

Pitching ace Dwight Gooden weighed in with some big numbers when he re-signed with the Mets in April 1991. The previous year teammate Darryl Strawberry had bagged a multimillion-dollar deal from the Dodgers.

Was Jordan overpaid? Ruth overpaid? Ali overpaid? No, because they made their sports. But what about the guy hitting .260 who gets paid millions?

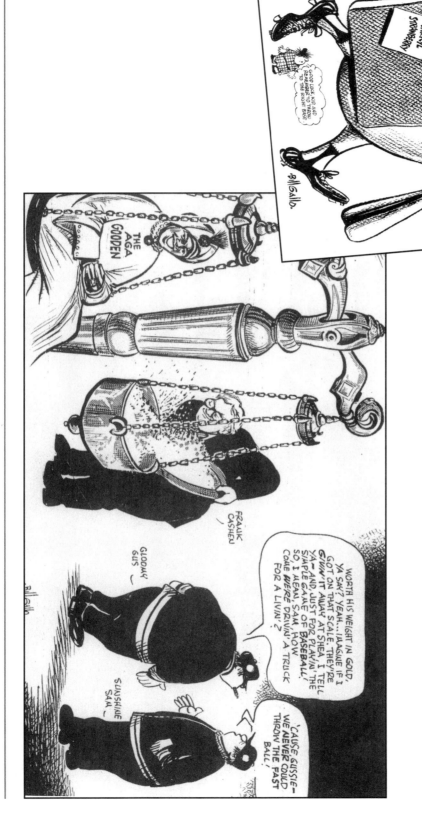

SEE MY AGENT

Somehow the players were much nicer, much easier to talk to, when they didn't make huge salaries. Athletes used to need newspapermen to generate publicity when they were on their way out.

Now, with all this money, there's no need for athletes to be good to the press. They can pay for good will—they have their agents, who are responsible for finding them ways to make money once their playing days are over.

Here's a small example of how we live in the age of the agent. When I used to run dinners for the National Cartoonists Society, I'd call up ballplayers directly, invite them to be guest speakers and they would come. Now they say, "Call my agent." And the agent says, "How much?" Hey, even Yuchie has an agent, now!

DOUGH BOYS

Over the years, I've shown the influence of big money on sports in a number of ways, in tones humorous and serious. I've sketched athletes holding up the owners, lounging in the lap of luxury, and saluting the Almighty Dollar.

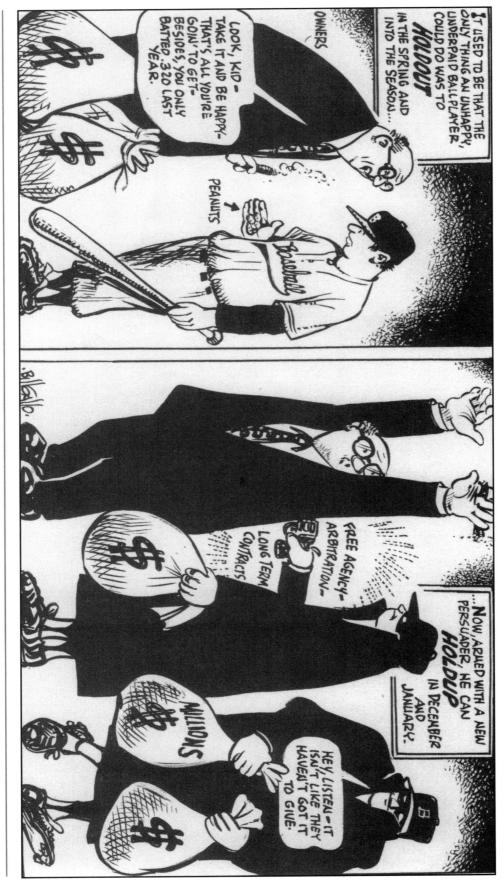

THE BIG PICTURE, MORE OR LESS

The illustration that best sums up the salary situation ran in December 1992. It juxtaposed two strikingly different news stories: free agent Barry Bonds had turned down the Yankees' five-year $38-million offer, even as people in Somalia were up against famine and starvation.

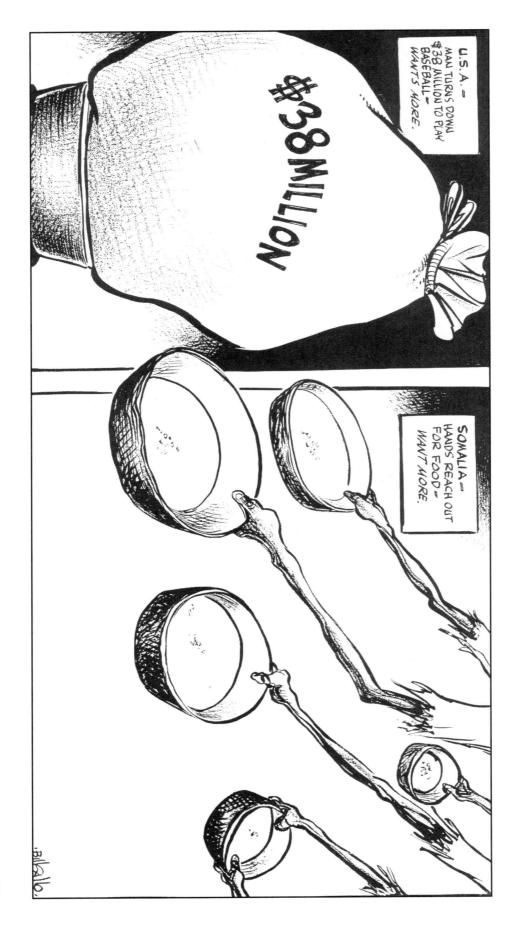

THE FLIP SIDE: TIME IS MONEY

Another thing that money tends to do is keep an athlete around too long. This, of course, predates huge salaries. Sugar Ray Robinson boxed until he was forty-four, and it wasn't like he had to prove anything. He simply needed the money.

Time, because they're allowed to do it. In baseball, you can't hang around if you can't do it anymore; nobody puts you on their team. But in boxing, it becomes a sideshow. The boxers get an opportunity for another payday when promoters—selfish promoters—know the man can't fight any-

more but figure he has some clout left at the box office.

After basketball's Bill Laimbeer called it quits in 1993, Father Time imparted the wisdom of the ancients to a couple of boxing Methuselahs, Larry Holmes and Roberto Duran.

FIGHT TO THE FINISH

When a fighter needs money, he fools himself that he still can do it. They're the last to know. Jack Dempsey and I were watching a bout once where somebody a little too old was fighting. I asked him about that, and he said, "It's in his mind. In his mind, he can still fight. In my mind, I can throw that left hook, and I throw it perfectly, and the man goes down. But it's only in my mind." He was in his seventies at the time.

Sugar Ray Robinson found himself in the headlock of a relentless opponent toward the end of his career. The mood was lighter and the fighters heavier in a 1990s drawing about an oft-proposed match between old-timers Larry Holmes and George Foreman.

WINNER IN A CAKEWALK

Father Time is undefeated over the long haul, but he doesn't win every contest. Jimmy Connors marked his fortieth birthday in 1992 by taking a match at the U.S. Open, the year after he had made a rousing run in the same tournament. I sent him this birthday greeting via *The News*.

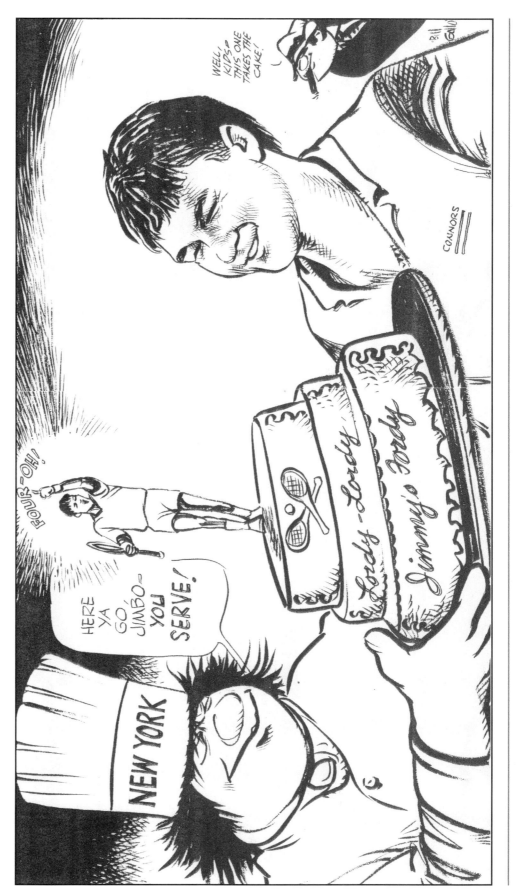

STOP THE CLOCK

As a forty-three-year-old quarterback and place kicker for the Oakland Raiders, George Blanda showed the kind of longevity that can inspire a second childhood.

CHAPTER SEVENTEEN

HOOP DREAMS

GO WEST

During the Knicks' playoff run to the NBA Finals in 1999, Madison Square Garden was packed, celebrity row was in session at courtside and scalpers were inflating ticket prices to four figures. Quite a different scene from when I first watched the Knicks, in the early 1950s. In those days, hardly anybody would be at their games. A co-worker and I would head over to the old Garden during our Saturday lunch break, flash a press ticket and sit behind the Knicks' bench. I'd try to catch them playing the Rochester Royals, because an old classmate of mine, Bobby Wanzer, played for that team.

This was before the three-point shot and twenty-four-second clock; foul shots were one-and-one, which meant you had to sink the first shot to get a second. Occasionally the Knicks' game would be paired with a Harlem Globetrotters' match, and then the place would be packed. The Globetrotters were so entertaining that people would sometimes watch them play and walk out on the Knick game.

It didn't take long for the NBA to develop some of that entertainment value itself and evolve into a major sport. By the late 1950s, it was pretty well on its way to becoming a faster, more inventive game. Bob Cousy and Dick McGuire were two of the fancy Dans who made the league exciting; Oscar Robertson could do everything and was a pleasure to watch. Then there were big scorers like Jerry West and Rick Barry. I illustrated the futility of trying to stop West in the 1970 NBA Finals, Knicks vs. Lakers.

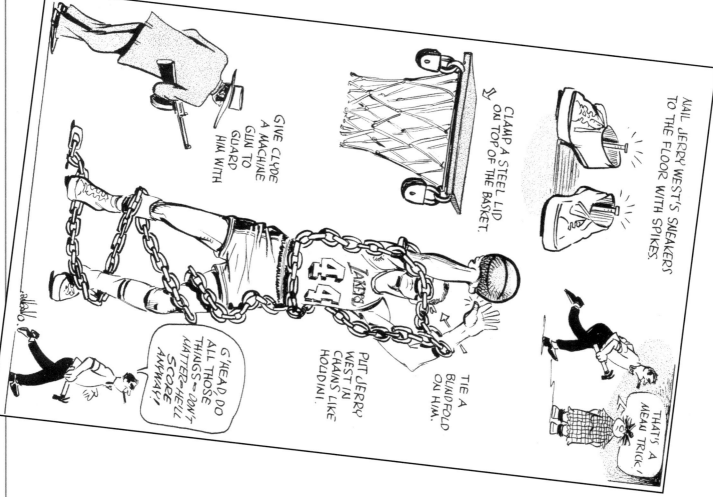

THE DOCTOR WILL SEE YOU NOW

Julius Erving wasn't the first pro to fly to the hoop like Peter Pan—Elgin Baylor had shown some of that, too, for the Lakers—but Doctor J amazed me more than anybody. (Anybody, that is, until a certain player came along on the Chicago Bulls.) Erving was a star in the old American Basketball Association before coming to the NBA, and in this drawing from January 1975 he goes airborne with the ABA's red-white-and-blue ball in hand.

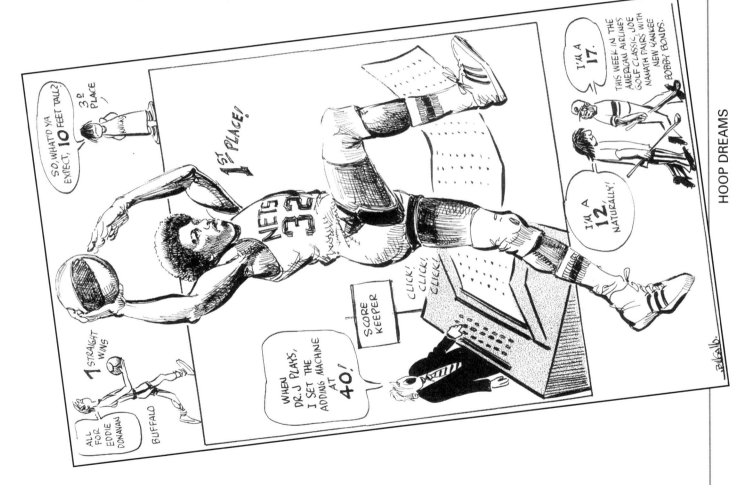

A BIRD IN THE HAND

Like Bob Cousy, Larry Bird brought a quarterback's vision and awareness to the court. After making a key steal to beat the Detroit Pistons in the playoffs in May 1987, I likened him to other legendary thieves (aka goniffs). Larry's many talents led me to imagine a flock of Birds on one team (with a nod to Hakeem Olajuwon of the Houston Rockets).

In the spring of 1973, I noted how a previous Celtic star, John Havlicek, also had the potential to stop a team dead in its tracks.

HOOP DREAMS

STILL WORKING THEIR MAGIC

Despite all the dazzling players who had come along, I hadn't forgotten about the Globetrotters. When Magic Johnson decided to take a team of his own on tour, I already knew of the perfect opponent and made that suggestion in December 1993.

THEY MIGHT BE GIANTS

The big thing with fans in the 1950s was the enormous height of the players. "Why don't they raise the baskets?" was a question asked by spectators who considered six-feet-two as being tall.

The view that the game was tilted toward the towering player showed up in my reaction to Wilt Chamberlain's 100-point effort against the Knicks in March 1962. And in this January 1968 drawing of Lew Alcindor, the UCLA star took up the entire length of a *News* sports page. The occasion? The pride of Power Memorial High School, now a collegian in California, was returning to New York to play at Madison Square Garden.

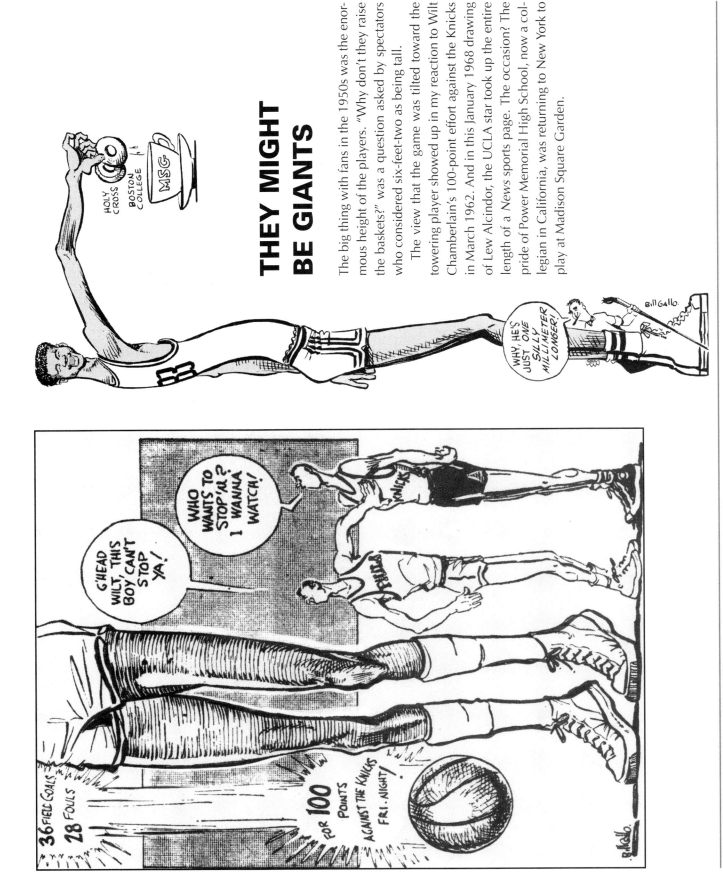

CENTERS OF ATTENTION

Almost four years later, in December 1971, I revisited Alcindor before one of the great regular-season clashes in NBA history. By then he was known as Kareem Abdul-Jabbar, center for the defending champion Milwaukee Bucks. Out in Los Angeles, Chamberlain and his Laker teammates were running off a colossal win streak. The two teams met in January 1972, and the Bucks snapped L.A.'s victory string at 33 games. The Lakers would not be denied come playoff time, though, and wound up taking the 1971–72 crown.

TOP BILLING

The way Bill Russell played defense was close to genius, and the big center led the Celtics to eleven championships in thirteen seasons in the 1950s and '60s. When this was drawn in February 1975, though, Russell was coach of the Seattle Super-Sonics and the center of some controversy for shunning induction into the Basketball Hall of Fame.

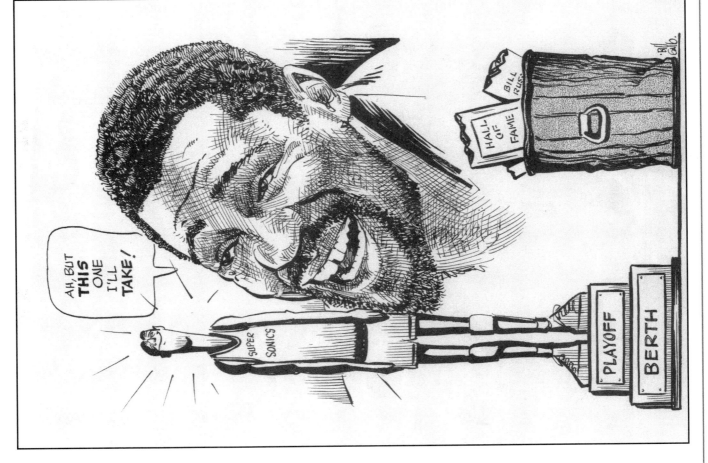

HOOP DREAMS

THOSE CHAMPIONSHIP SEASONS

En route to a pair of NBA titles, the Knicks of the early '70s combined the talents of exceptional players like forward Dave DeBusschere, a source of steady support for the team, and guard Walt Frazier, a flashy figure off the court and a defensive star on it. In January 1972, shortly after a huge heist at

New York's Hotel Pierre, I compared Walt to an Old West thief for his ball-stealing savvy. A night was held in his honor at the Garden in December 1979, and Frazier, aka Clyde, was dressed for the occasion in my cartoon.

USING HIS HEAD

Bill Bradley was the Knicks' Rhodes scholar, but I suggested he add to his reading list after an on-court fight with Rick Barry in February 1975. Senator Bradley had a book out himself in 1996, about the time beleaguered Knick coach Don Nelson needed a few words of wisdom.

A WINNING COMBINATION

Red Auerbach always claims that his Celtics were the best congregation in basketball, and a lot of people would agree. But basketball experts also would agree that the Knicks of 1969–70 were the epitome of a team. Each of them made the others look better, and that's what a good team does. I reassembled that starting five—Clyde Frazier, Dick Barnett, Willis Reed, Dave DeBusschere and Dollar Bill Bradley—during the 1980s to look over a latter-day team coached by Rick Pitino.

THE BIG RED ONE

But the real star of the champion Knick teams of the '70s was Red Holzman, the coach who knew how to weave all the talent together. I showed him as the leader of the band (playing a Reed, as in his

MVP center, Willis Reed) when the Knicks won their first title, in May 1970. And I fondly remembered Holzman upon his death in November 1998.

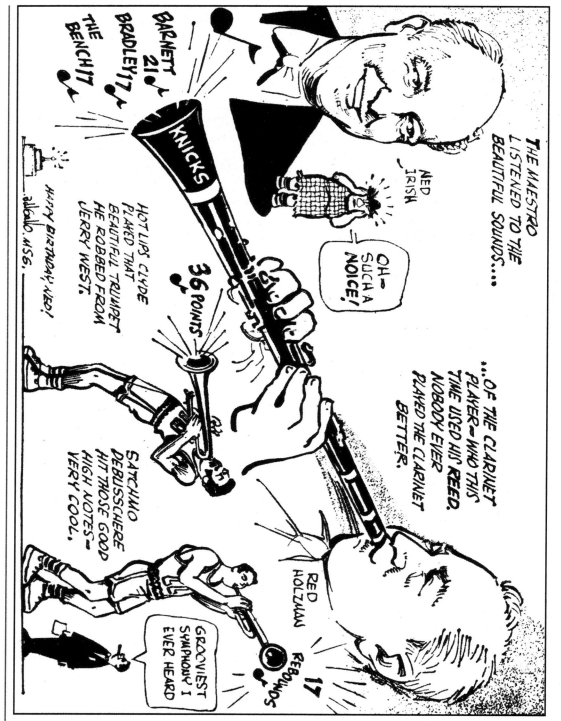

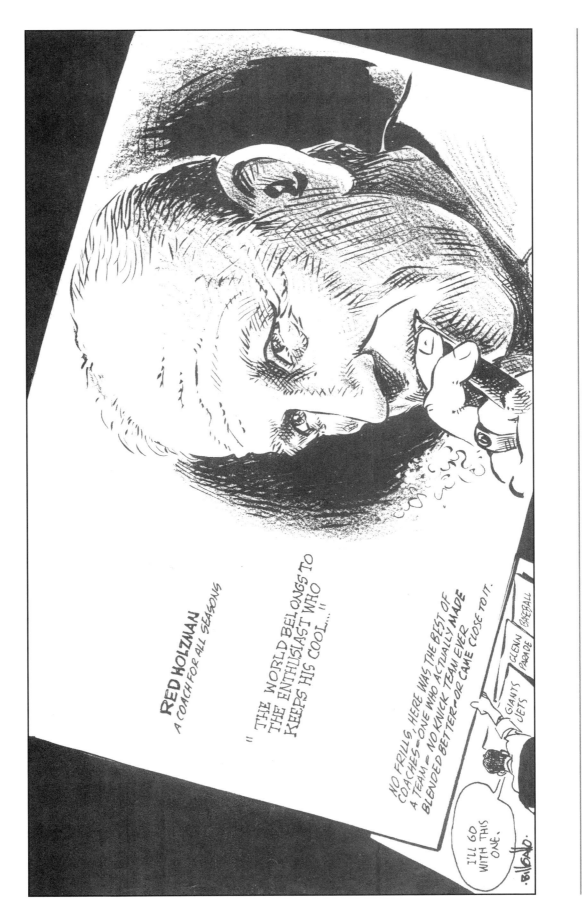

HE'S NO. 1

In my estimation, Michael Jordan was the perfect athlete. He did so many phenomenal things, you started to expect it of him. You stopped saying, "Wow," and you started saying, "Of course, it's Michael Jordan." He personifies excellence and is the kind of athlete who lifts everyone around him.

Of all the great athletes I've seen, Jordan is the greatest, as I explain below. In fact, I had him rated No. 1 overall in March 1995, when he returned to basketball after a stint in baseball—and that was before he led the Bulls to three more titles.

HERE I GIVE YOU THE GREATEST IN EACH SPORT THAT I'VE EVER SEEN —MY OPINION. WHAT I'VE SET OUT TO DO IS TO PICK THE ONE AMONGST THESE GREATS—THE ONE I CHOOSE (MY OPINION) AS, "THE GREATEST OF ALL ATHLETES I'VE EVER SEEN" (MY TIME).

AS FAR AS I'M CONCERNED, NOBODY WAS EVER AS GREAT AS JIM BROWN IN PRO FOOTBALL. →

IN BASEBALL MY CHOICE IS JOE DIMAGGIO— I SAW NONE BETTER ON A BASEBALL FIELD.

THE BEST FIGHTER, NO QUESTION, WAS SUGAR RAY ROBINSON →

I SEE WAYNE GRETZKY AS HOCKEY'S NUMBER ONE...

PRO BASKETBALL HAD A LIST OF CANDIDATES FOR ME—THEN ALONG CAME MISTER JORDAN. HE IS THE BEST EVER (MY OPINION) AT THIS DEMANDING SPORT— AND (IN MY BOOK)— THE NUMBER 1 ATHLETE—"THE GREATEST OF ALL ATHLETES I'VE EVER SEEN," THE OTHER FOUR PICTURED HERE ARE TIED FOR 2ª.

ANY ARGUMENTS? Bill Gallo.

HERE COMES MR. JORDAN

My wife likes the ballet, so I said to her, "Come on, we're going to the ballet. We're not going to see Baryshnikov, but Jordan."

During that game, the Knicks were getting on Jordan, really letting him have it. Then he got to the foul line . . . and shut his eyes. He made sure the Knicks saw him. And, with his eyes closed, Michael Jordan sank the foul shots. He didn't laugh or smile. He just went about his business.

This drawing doesn't capture his grace on the court, but it does show his power and determination.

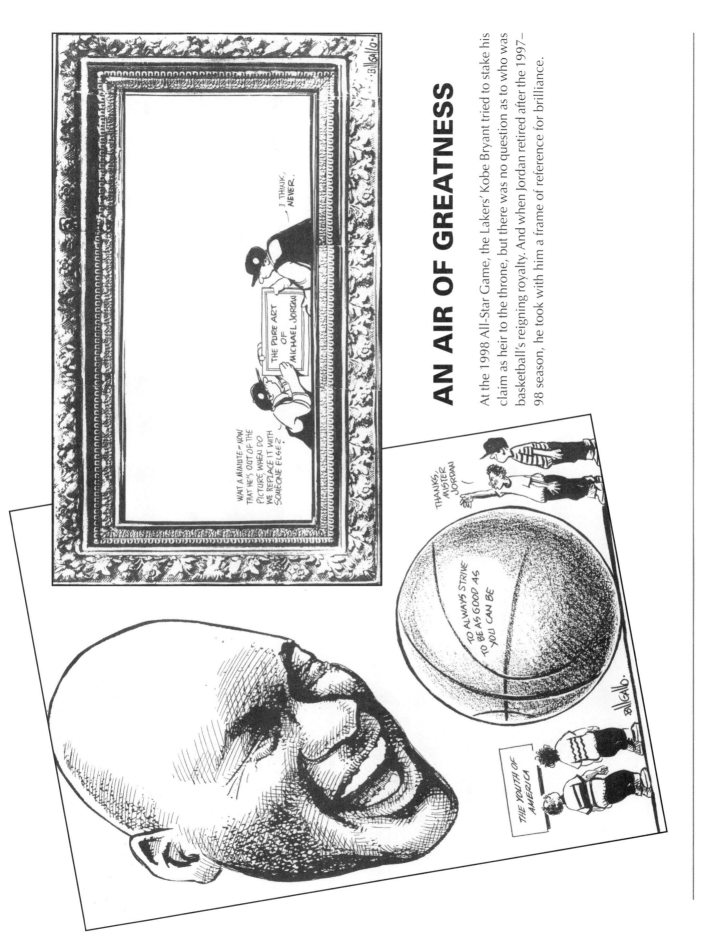

AN AIR OF GREATNESS

At the 1998 All-Star Game, the Lakers' Kobe Bryant tried to stake his claim as heir to the throne, but there was no question as to who was basketball's reigning royalty. And when Jordan retired after the 1997–98 season, he took with him a frame of reference for brilliance.

SHOOTING STAR

"Pistol" Pete Maravich was a hugely talented and flashy player, and he left Louisiana State University as college's all-time scorer. His trademark long hair and sloppy socks added to his appeal, as did his spectacular passes and between-the-legs dribble. He played right out of the schoolyard, but with more finesse. And he was so dedicated to the game. His style inspired a lot of kids—and the contract he signed with the Atlanta Hawks in 1970 inspired their dads.

TAKING AIM

In March 1970, at the end of his college career, Maravich came to the Garden to play in the NIT. He had an off game against Georgetown, although his team narrowly won. A few days later, I juxtaposed the hopeful gaze of Maravich with the icy assessment of his father, Press Maravich, Pete's coach at LSU. When you get a quote like that, you use it.

In February 1977, playing for the New Orleans Jazz, Maravich riddled the Knicks for 68 points in one game. To show what Pistol Pete had inflicted on the New York squad, I reprised the slumped figure of Lee Marvin's drunken cowboy in the 1965 movie *Cat Ballou*.

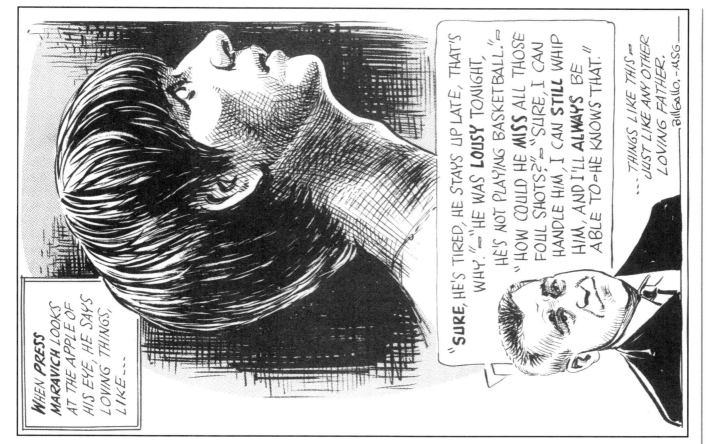

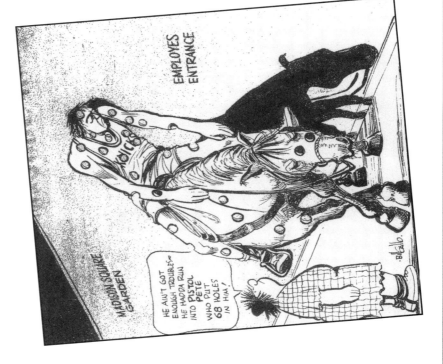

PETE'S SAKE

I used to feel bad for Maravich. I had met him a couple of times and found him hard to talk to. He would shy away from people. Then I read about him. His old man was tough, and Pete had to please him. Yet it's ironic that if his father wasn't the person he was, Pete wouldn't have been great. I saw a sensitivity in Maravich. He was just one

of those athletes you focus on. You try to figure out what makes him tick, figure out the kind of character that drives a guy to throw so much into one thing. He looked bothered . . . and those people interest me. This was my remembrance of Pistol Pete when he died of a heart attack in January 1988, at the age of forty.

FINDING A WAY

In the spring of 1999, the Knicks were in danger of missing the playoffs with just eight games left in a strike-shortened season. The general manager had been fired, and the same fate seemed to loom over Jeff Van Gundy, the team's young coach. Phil Jackson, the one-time Knicks player who had gone on to coach the Chicago Bulls to a half dozen titles, was seen as waiting in the wings for Van Gundy's job.

Was there a way out of this hairy situation? Looking to Knicks star Latrell Sprewell, I mapped a few routes for a possible playoff drive.

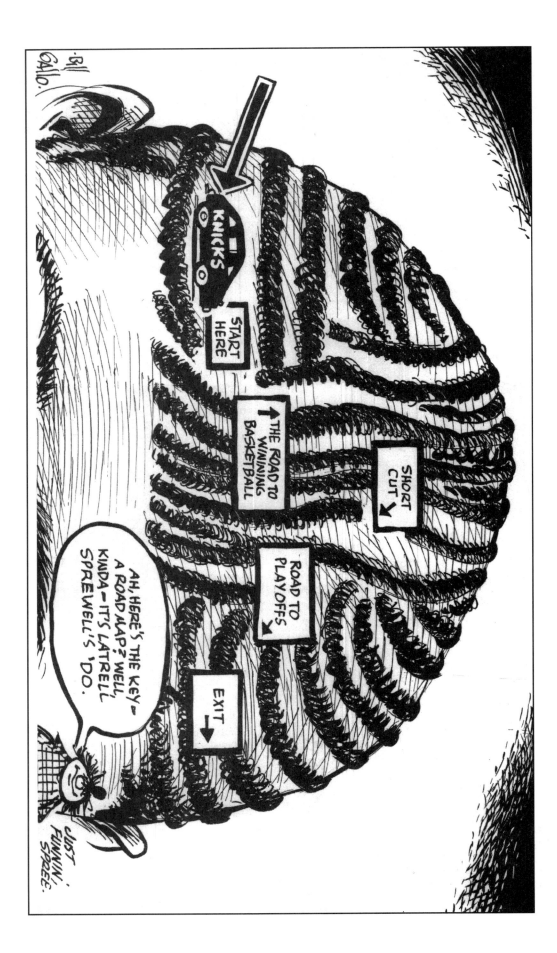

A BRAND-NEW START OF IT

Sprewell had a troubled history, but as I had noted upon his joining the Knicks that season, New York believes in second chances.

GIVE 'EM A RUN FOR THEIR MONEY

"ROCKY" . . . THE SAGA BEGINS

Now no one will ever confuse Jeff Van Gundy with Sylvester Stallone. Still, that spring Van Gundy got top billing in my own "Rocky" serial, which unfolded over two months—from the conclusion of the regular season through the NBA Finals. The story actually began with a late-season Knicks win over Pat Riley's Miami Heat. In that, I saw the beginnings of an underdog success story.

ROUND ONE

As the conference's eighth-place team, the Knicks opened against the top seed, the Miami Heat, and their coach, aka Hotstuff. Not long before, Pat Riley had been the Knicks' coach himself, but he had left for Miami in 1995 and was now the enemy. With this illustration, I answered those who questioned my casting decision.

GIVE 'EM A RUN FOR THEIR MONEY

TAKING SOME HEAT

While the slick-dressing Riley (aka "Armani") landed a few blows, the eventual outcome of the series didn't suit him: the Knicks, led by Allan Houston and Patrick Ewing, floored Miami to move on to a postseason sequel.

GIVE 'EM A RUN FOR THEIR MONEY

ROUND TWO

The New Yorkers raced through the next round, a series against the Atlanta Hawks, and were suddenly on a collision course with the Indiana Pacers. Amid the excitement, I called a timeout to see if Madison Square Garden president Dave Checketts might be having some second thoughts about letting go his general manager, Ernie Grunfeld.

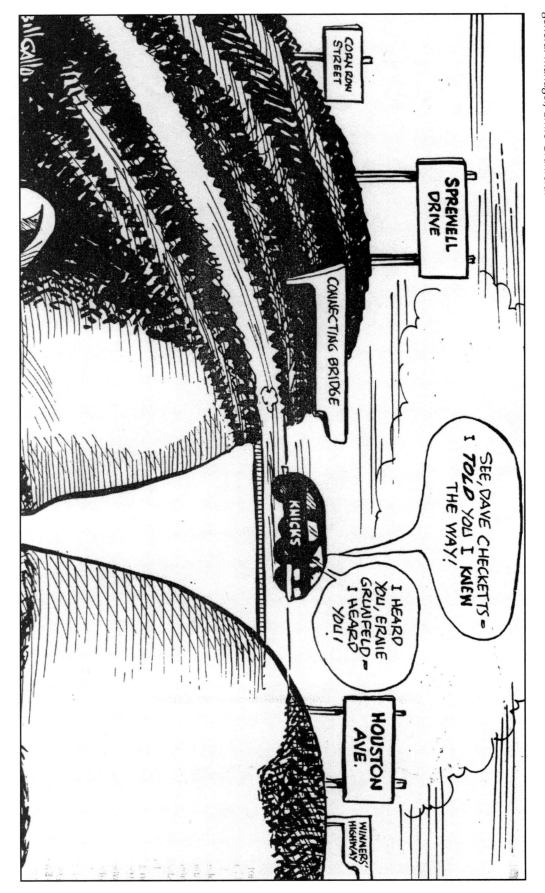

GIVE 'EM A RUN FOR THEIR MONEY

ROUND THREE

Then came the heavily favored Pacers, coached by former Celtics great Larry Bird. The teams split the first four games, generating a new round of suspense—particularly when the Knicks lost their star "big guy" center, Ewing, to injury for the rest of the year.

FEATHER IN THEIR CAP

Despite being shorthanded, the Knicks captured Games Five and Six from Bird's squad, and for the first time in the league's half-century history, an eighth-place team had made it to the NBA Finals.

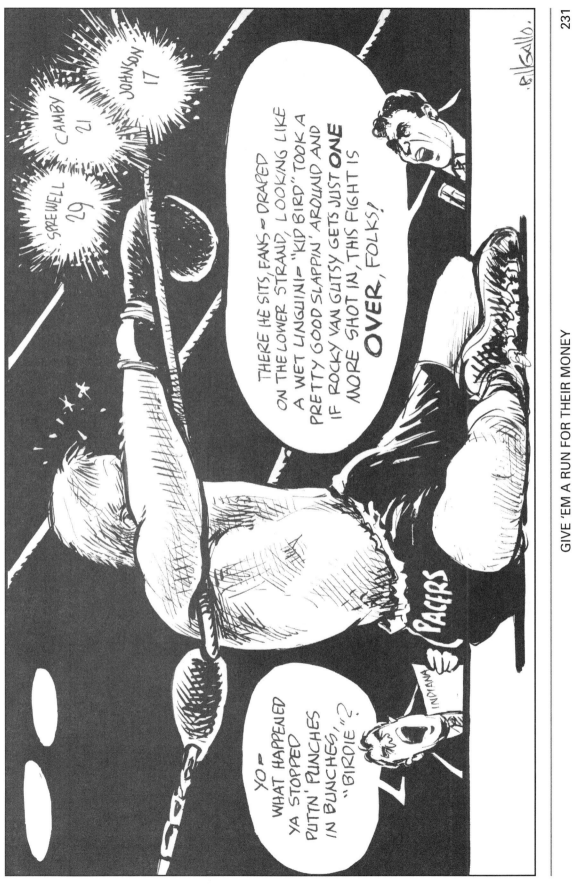

GIVE 'EM A RUN FOR THEIR MONEY

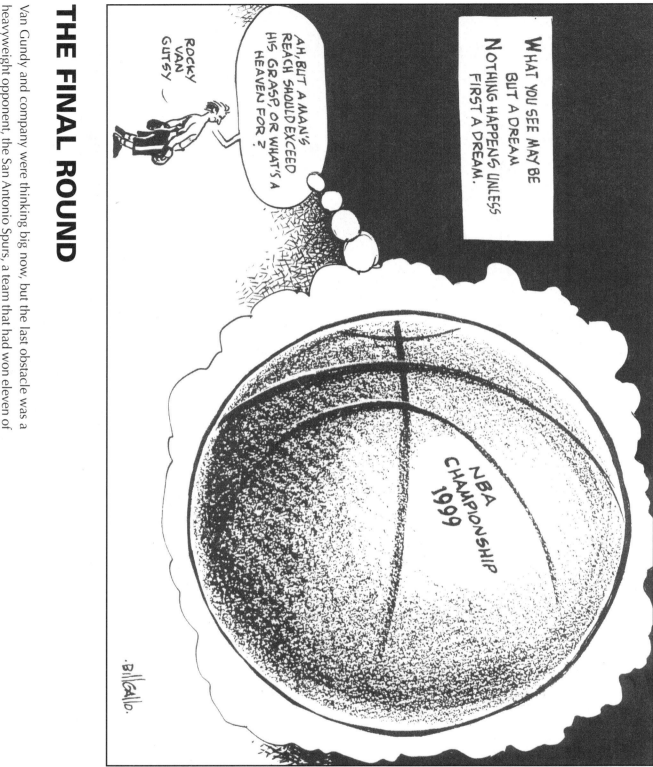

THE FINAL ROUND

Van Gundy and company were thinking big now, but the last obstacle was a heavyweight opponent, the San Antonio Spurs, a team that had won eleven of twelve playoff games. In Rocky's dressing room, the drama was building.

SPURRED ON

Spurs coach Gregg Popovich became "Ol' Popo" for my purposes, and he had quite an arsenal at his disposal, particularly stars Tim Duncan and David Robinson. The Knicks dropped the first two games of the series, and for the first time in the playoffs appeared outgunned.

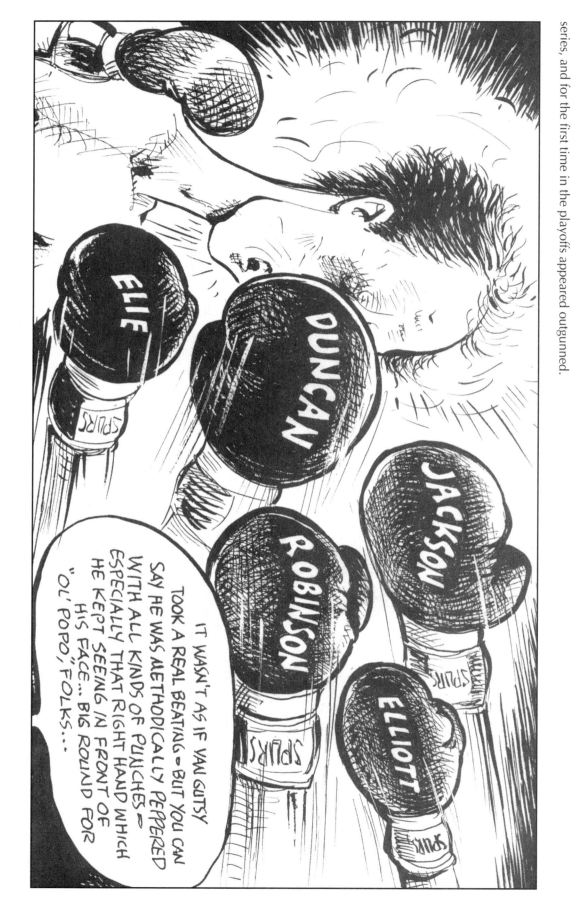

GOING DOWN SWINGING

Van Gutsy still had plenty of fight in him and threw one more haymaker, in Game Three. The Spurs wrapped up the NBA championship in the next two games, but in the end the Knicks and their coach had demonstrated their character.

GIVE 'EM A RUN FOR THEIR MONEY

DRAWING A CROWD

CHAPTER NINETEEN

CAUSE CELEBS

CARY-ED AWAY

Celebrities often mosey into our sports neighborhood, and then they become part of the story. This drawing of Cary Grant, however, was a scene of my own devising.

It started when Sandy Koufax and Don Drysdale jointly held out for more money before the Dodgers' 1966 season. Seeking leverage in the standoff, the two pitchers announced that they had struck a deal to become movie actors and would make their fortune on the screen. In that case, I figured it was only right for the Dodgers to look to Hollywood to fill the team's pitching needs. So I fitted Cary Grant for an L.A. uniform (after finding out that he was a left-hander).

The plot thickened when my cartoon caught the eye of Frank Sinatra. He requested the original as a gift to Grant, and I happily obliged. A typed, signed letter on Cary Grant's letterhead soon followed. Dated April 12, 1966, it read in part:

I was extremely flattered by your cartoon. Several people sent it to me from New York. Please try to join my wife and me at the game just to see if Walter O'[Malley] or Buzz Bavasi [the Dodgers' general manager] have put your suggestion into effect. It would certainly surprise everyone. Most of all me.

DEAR WALTER O'MALLEY,
SINCE YOU ARE TEMPORARILY LOSING TWO PITCHERS TO THE MOVIES, WHY NOT GET THIS FELLA TO DO SOME OF YOUR PITCHING? HE WON'T WIN MANY GAMES, BUT HE'LL PACK 'EM IN ON LADIES' DAY! THINK ABOUT IT.
REGARDS,
Bill Gallo

THE SINGING WAITER

That Cary Grant cartoon wasn't the last of my illustrations to be enjoyed by Frank Sinatra. In November of 1978, the singer was chairman (fittingly enough) of a Joe Louis benefit, $500 a plate at Caesars Palace in Las Vegas. Sinatra was close to Joe, and he knew that the former heavyweight champ needed help. In my drawing of the event, I made Frank a waiter at the dinner.

Sinatra got a big kick out of it and asked for the original, which I sent him. Not long after, I received a response:

The drawing is great and you're great too for being so thoughtful. I kind of like the idea of being portrayed as a waiter at Caesars Palace... If the pipes quit on me, I might take the job.

It was signed simply "Francis." I received four letters from Sinatra over the years, and they were all signed that way or "Francis Albert."

STEALING THE BALL

The Watergate drama and the world of pro sports met in the person of Lawrence O'Brien, who headed the Democratic National Committee at the time of the Washington break-in and a few years later was named commissioner of the National Basketball Association. I seized on this connection for a cartoon, which I sent along to O'Brien. His handwritten reply, dated May 20, 1975, made reference to the Nixon era's Committee to Reelect the President (CREEP) and to his new basketball post:

It [the drawing] really was to the point and brought back some not-so-fond thoughts of Watergate and those CREEPS.

I appreciate the cartoon, Bill, and you have given me a pleasant start on what I know is a difficult task.

TOP-RANKED

It is no secret that real estate mogul Donald Trump has a very healthy ego (see page 60). But even with his many business interests, he's found time to write when I've included him in one of my cartoons.

Take the one I did in September 1983, after Trump bought the New Jersey Generals of the (now-defunct) United States Football League. The following month, he graciously sent me a note to express his appreciation. "I am delighted to have it," he added. "Keep up the great work. . . . My dad and I are longtime fans."

SOUP'S ON

Gagster Soupy Sales, who enjoyed a huge burst of popularity in the mid-'60s with his kids show, knows the comic value of a good pie in the face. I put that skill to use in this May 1965 drawing. It takes a jab at Sonny Liston's first-round flop against Muhammad Ali in their rematch, held two days before.

Soupy quickly dropped me a line about his guest appearance:

I can't tell you how flattered I was to see your sketch involving me in Thursday's Daily News. I'm doubly flattered because I've been a big fan of yours for a long time.

He added this postscript:

Sonny Liston was my mother's name!!!

TRUTH BE TOLD

On the hot seat for reneging on his "no new taxes" pledge, President George Bush made a guest appearance in this July 1990 cartoon, a takeoff on the old TV program *To Tell the Truth*. At the end of the month I heard from Mark Goodson, the game-show's producer, asking if he might buy the original. (I wound up giving him a copy.)

People featured in my cartoons often ask for the original artwork. If possible, I'm happy to oblige, but I can't be as accommodating when the requests come from the public at large. Collecting sports memorabilia has become big business, and I've found that people sometimes request a cartoon, then turn around and sell it. They don't really care about the drawing; they're just interested in the dollar sign.

GOING THROUGH CHANNELS

Sometimes I visit the celebs on their turf. In 1970, I bypassed the ballfield and went to Lincoln Center to interview dancer Edward Villella. I had heard him mention on *The Tonight Show* that he was a boxer before taking up ballet. I never saw Villella box, but they tell me he was pretty good. So I requested an interview with him and wound up featuring him in a photo essay, under the heading "Ballet in Sweat Socks," which illustrated the parallels between an athlete's moves and a ballet dancer's.

That story additionally earned me the honor of being kicked out of Lincoln Center by none other than George Balanchine. The famous choreographer came upon me during my discussion with Villella and wanted to know what I was up to. When he learned that a sportswriter was taking up his dancer's time, he booted me from the premises, intoning, "Out! Out! Out!"

The Villella piece didn't use drawings, but in the late '70s I opened my sketchbook to *News* readers and warned those familiar faces on TV that they were being watched—and drawn into my sphere of interest.

"HOLD STILL, I'M DRAWING!"

—BY BILL GALLO

LISTEN ALL YOU TV stars who come into my living room, you are being watched. I'm looking at you with pen and pad in hand and I'm studying your contours, your every expression. I'm sketching furiously, and you are my captive models. Some artists have to pay for models, but me, I get mine for free.

Being a sports cartoonist, I'm always warming up—like a pitcher in the bullpen or even a piano player going through the scales before he plays Mozart.

Some people, I'm told, do the crossword puzzle while watching "Mork and Mindy," and others read a book and view the set at the same time. But me, I have this compulsion to sketch whoever comes on the tube.

So if you're reading this, President Carter, next time sit still and don't look so apprehensive. Remember: somebody, somewhere is sketching you.

THE ART OF THE MATTER

Norman Rockwell was one of the greats, although he was never regarded that way by the somewhat stuffy critics. I think they were all wrong, and that they realize it now. Rockwell was a storyteller—he told the story of America in his day—and will be seen as an even greater artist as time passes.

This portrait, which I drew on request, was presented to Rockwell as part of a day-long salute to the artist in his hometown.

A SWELL BUNCH

Celebrities tend to be basketball fans, and that's because the camera is on them a lot in that setting. I'm not criticizing them. That's their business: to promote themselves and be seen.

Besides, they're legitimate fans. Most of them are animated during the game, although Woody Allen is so stoic you can't tell if he's rooting or not. Another exception is Peter Falk, who also happens

to be quite an artist. I met him at a billiard tournament and found him to be a quiet, subdued guy who doesn't pursue the limelight.

At the conclusion of the NBA players' strike in January 1999, the celebs—including their unofficial captain, Spike Lee—were set to reclaim their courtside seats.

A DIALOGUE WITH HEPBURN

I once tangled with Katharine Hepburn, though not face-to-face. I was watching the Oscar winner in the play *West Side Waltz* in 1982 when, during the performance, she noticed that a front-row spectator had put his feet up on the stage as if it were his own personal hassock. "*You must take your feet* off the stage!" she commanded. At the curtain call, she resumed telling the fellow off, so much so that the embarrassed man actually walked out with his head bowed. Meanwhile, Hepburn's point had been lost amid her overreaction. So I had Bertha answer her in this cartoon.

ON THE AISLE FOR ANNIE

The outcome was much more pleasant when Bertha got to review the musical Annie. Shelly Bruce, then playing the title role, stopped by my office with her mother after this drawing ran in 1978.

HELLO, BERTHA!

Once the Mets had become world champs in 1969, Bertha even toyed with a stage career herself. Since she owed her existence to the last-place finish of those early Mets, the team's newfound glory posed a threat to her very identity. I suggested that she follow in the footsteps of Pearl Bailey (herself a well-known Mets fan) and star in *Hello, Dolly!*

LAUNCHING PAD

John Glenn was a different sort of celebrity, a huge hero when he circled Earth during the early days of the space program. New York honored him with a ticker-tape parade, and he was treated to a second one upon his return to space in 1998. This portrait appeared in *The News* on the day of Glenn's first parade, in March 1962—minus the autograph. A colleague who was working for WPIX television caught up with the astronaut on his big day and got him to add that finishing touch.

SPEAKING OF HOWARD

I knew Howard Cosell a long time, right from the beginning, when he would walk around with his tape recorder and tape athletes in the dugout. His boxing recaps with Ali and his stint in the broadcast booth for *Monday Night Football* were still to come.

Cosell used to give me the business, and I suspect it was largely because of his feud with my friend Dick Young of *The News*. When he looked at me, he saw Dick Young. Cosell and I were on the same flight once when he suddenly exclaimed, "Oh, my God! I just had a terrible thought! If I die before Dick Young, he'll write a terrible obituary about me." (As it turned out, Young died well before Cosell did.)

Of course, Howard didn't like some of the digs in my drawings of him, especially if it concerned his toupee. But to me, he was entertainment and grist for my mill, such as when *Monday Night Football* took a ratings hit from an airing of *The Godfather* or when I likened that broadcast team to the Three Stooges (with Dandy Don Meredith and Frank Gifford filling out the trio). Cosell was fair game, and he walked right into it.

WHAT IS A HOWARD COSELL?
—BY
— BILL GALLO

DRAWING A CROWD

CAUSE CELEBS

IT'S UP TO YOU, NY NY

I had heard that Frank Sinatra was a difficult man, but upon interviewing him in 1983, I found him easy to be around. There was a pleasantry about him that was appealing.

He was well-versed on boxing, which was the occasion for our meeting. Sinatra was going to do color commentary for an upcoming fight in the South African region known as Bophuthatswana, and his PR man, Lee Solters, asked Frank if he would sit for an interview with some sports writers. Sinatra agreed—but only if it was me and UPI sports editor Milt Richman.

The chat was to take place at New Jersey's Meadowlands sports arena, where the vocalist was giving a concert, and the toughest part of our get-together was penetrating all the layers of security surrounding Frank. I was taken by limousine to the arena, where we pulled behind a silver-and-black limo with the license plate "NY NY." Inside the building, I was escorted by two burly bodyguards into a waiting room; I was checked over and sent into another room. I was then ushered into an empty dressing room, and it was there that the Chairman of the Board made his entrance wearing a Mets baseball jacket.

The subsequent story, "Sinatra at Ringside," ran in the *Daily News* on April 23, 1983. In his own words, Ol' Blue Eyes recalled how he had been a fight fan since the age of five, when he was given boxing gloves as a present, and had once dreamed of becoming a boxer. He ranked Sugar Ray Robinson, Willie Pep, Joe Louis and Rocky Marciano as his top four fighters, and singled out the Basilio-Robinson contest of March 25, 1958, as the best match he had ever seen.

Frank cherished memories of heading over to the old Madison Square Garden to watch the bouts. "I never missed a Friday night," he reminisced. "The great fights I saw there and the great times I had I wouldn't trade for anything. Going to the Friday night fights was an event, a great event."

The last time I saw Sinatra was at Carnegie Hall a few years before he died. My wife and I were lucky enough to be invited by Frank himself. What he didn't wind up doing with his fists in a boxing ring, Sinatra did with his voice in concert—he knocked 'em all out.

Here's my tribute to Frank following his death in 1998.

THE FINAL CURTAIN

FRANK SINATRA
1915 - 1998

CHAPTER TWENTY

TOUCH 'EM ALL

MEET ME IN ST. LOUIS

On my block in Astoria, it was almost a sin not to root for a New York baseball team. A kid would pull for the Yankees, Dodgers or Giants—well, most kids did. My team was the St. Louis Cardinals, a secret that I used to share with only my closest friends.

I later wondered why I was the only Cardinal fan I knew. Did others not see the things I saw in them? Hell, I thought, look at this ragamuffin team. Don't they symbolize the times? We were in the middle of the Depression, and people were scrambling to get by, relying on a never-say-die attitude.

I saw a similar spirit in those Cardinals of the 1930s. They were a bunch of guys with dirty uniforms, looking like poor kids coming into a rich neighborhood and outplaying a team of well-groomed showoffs. The Gashouse Gang, they were called. Perfect. We lived near a gashouse in Astoria.

My heroes were guys like Dizzy Dean and his brother Paul (aka Daffy), Pepper Martin and Joe (Ducky) Medwick. When they won the pennant in 1934, player-manager Frankie Frisch had five .300 hitters plus the Dean brothers on the mound. Frisch himself was a scrappy little guy dubbed the Fordham Flash.

The Cards played the Detroit Tigers in the World Series that year and won it in seven games, with Dizzy and Daffy Dean winning all four games, two apiece. The newspaper headlines, quoting Dizzy, read: "Me and Paul."

I loved all those colorful nicknames and enjoyed how they played "pepper" between games of a doubleheader, standing in a circle and doing tricks with the ball like the Globetrotters would do with a basketball. In these two drawings, I revisited the Gashouse Gang and dared to reveal a rooting interest for the Cards to meet the Yanks in the 1996 World Series.

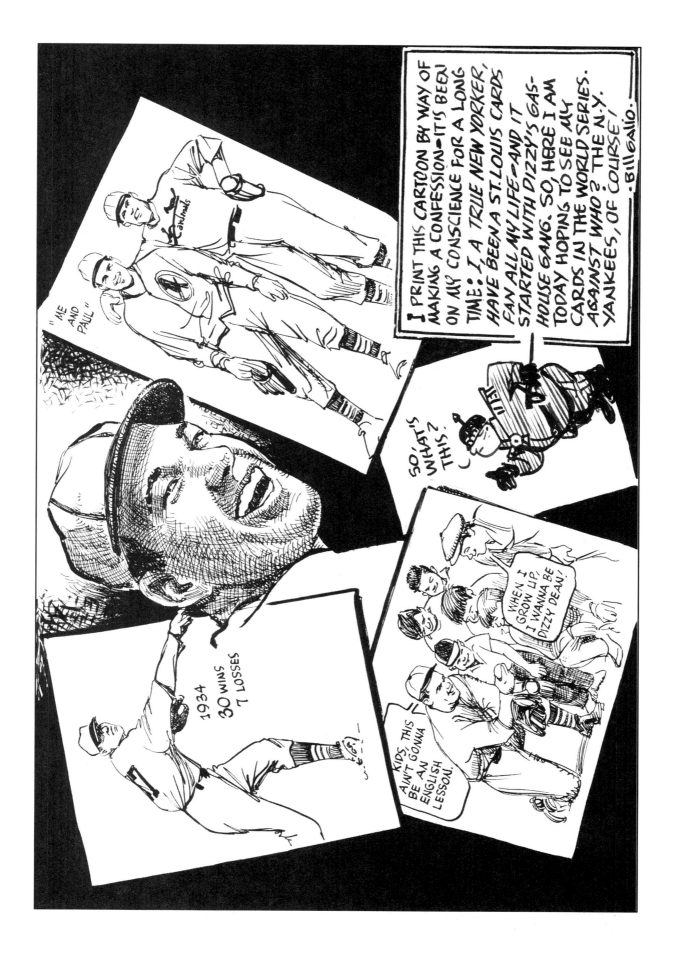

MY FINE
FEATHERED FRIENDS

Over the years, the Cardinals added to that legacy. Stan "The Man" Musial was one of the greatest ballplayers I ever saw; I particularly remember the Sunday doubleheader in which he belted five home runs. When he announced his retirement in 1963 after twenty-two seasons, I listed some of his accomplishments.

Bob Gibson was one of the top money pitchers of the 1960s, winning the seventh game in both the 1964 and 1967 World Series. I saluted him (and Johnny Mize) when he entered the Hall of Fame in 1981. His induction into Cooperstown provided a welcome lift following that summer's season-splitting baseball strike.

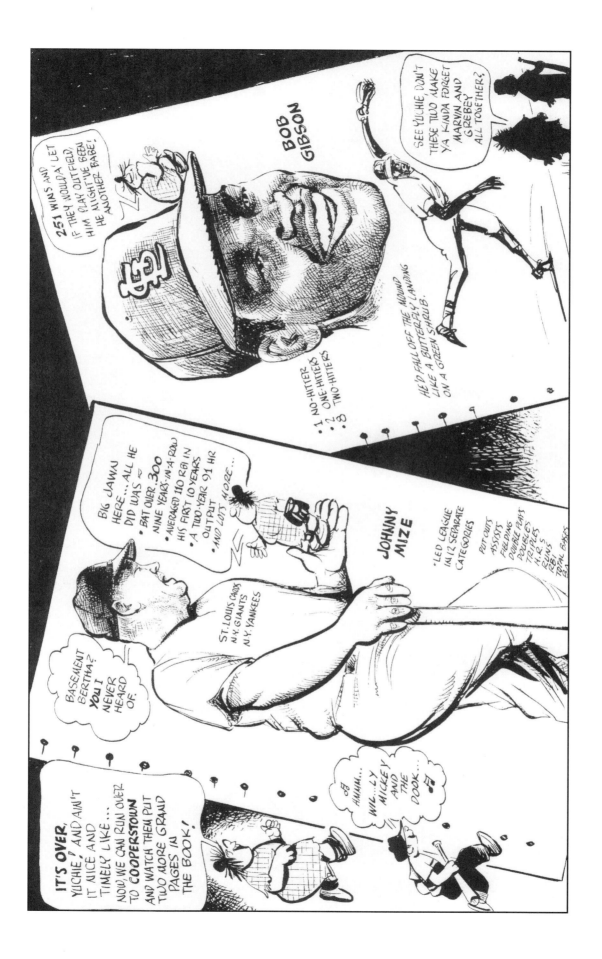

HORNS OF PLENTY

In 1958 I hit upon an idea that would become a *News* sports tradition: the awarding, in print, of a hero's wreath and goat horns to two deserving players after each World Series game. Baseball fans are usually curious about who rises to the occasion in the Series, and if there's a hero, I reasoned, there's a goat as well.

Still, I wasn't *The News*' official sports cartoonist at the time, and I didn't want to step on the toes of the person who was, Leo O'Mealia. So I went to Leo and asked, "Do you mind if I submit this idea?" He said, "No, go right ahead." The managing editor liked it too, and when we went ahead with it, *The News* received a lot of favorable mail. I even got a nice bonus. We were off and running.

The Braves' Warren Spahn was the first to wear the laurel wreath, for the first game of the '58 Series, but I didn't pick the first goat until the following day. Yanks pitcher Bob Turley had that dubious distinction, but he needn't have fretted. The Yanks came back to win that World Series, and Turley was my pick for the hero of Games Five and Seven.

Two years later, Pirates infielder Bill Mazeroski and Yankees pitcher Jim Coates divvied up the awards following the decisive game of the 1960 Fall Classic.

LEW BURDETTE   BOB TURLEY

BILL MAZEROSKI   JIM COATES

GETTING THEIR GOAT

After his playing days were over, Mickey Mantle confessed that he always worried about being fit for those goat horns. "You came close a couple of times," I informed him, and Mick got a kick out of that.

A teammate of Mantle's, Elston Howard, did get stuck with those horns, and he was a little hurt by it. He felt he didn't deserve it—but, sorry to say, I thought he did on that particular day. We remained friends, though.

Before the 1961 World Series, opposing managers Fred Hutchinson of the Reds and Ralph Houk of the Yankees surveyed my handiwork. By 1986, I had expanded the awards to include the National League Championship Series. In Game Five of that contest, the Mets' Gary Carter singled in the winning run off the Astros' Charlie Kerfeld, and my designations were made accordingly.

Strange as it may seem, some fans want to know in advance who's going to be the hero and who's going to be the goat!

GAME NO. 5
By BILL GALLO

HERO   GOAT

GARY CARTER   CHARLIE KERFELD

LOOK AT THE HORNS, RALPH!

YEA, FREDDIE—AND THE LAURELS!

GAME NO. 1

HERO   GOAT

..I'LL CHEW TIN CANS IF THE YANKEES DON'T TAKE IT IN....

...5 GAMES!

NO PASSING THE BUC

One of the more famous World Series heroes was Bill Mazeroski, who won the 1960 Fall Classic for the Pittsburgh Pirates over the Yankees with a home run in the bottom of the ninth inning in the seventh game.

I tried to anticipate the outcome of that contest and had to do some fast revisions when Mazeroski connected. That homer taught me a valuable lesson about keeping an open mind until the event is finished—to take Yogi's advice that it ain't over till it's over. The temptation is to jump the gun out of fear that an idea won't arrive in time for deadline, but your mind won't betray you like that. Besides, a drawing done beforehand is never spontaneous, and I like spontaneity.

THE KING OF CLOUT

What I find amazing about Hank Aaron is that he amassed 755 home runs in his career without ever hitting 50 in a season. Hammerin' Hank set an incredibly steady pace of 40 or so home runs a year.

FRONT AND CENTER

If baseball is the national pastime, New York for years played a spinoff game called "Who's the Best Center Fielder?" The contestants were Mickey Mantle of the Yankees, Willie Mays of the New York/San Francisco Giants and Duke Snider of the Brooklyn Dodgers. The subject was always on tap for a barroom debate, and even after the Duke faded from the scene, the argument stretched from the 1950s into the mid-'60s. In fact, I revived it in March 1985 when baseball commissioner Peter Ueberroth lifted the banishment of Mantle and Mays, exiled because of the PR work they did for casinos.

My pick for No. 1 would be Mays. He was the more rounded, more exciting ballplayer. Second was Mantle.

SAY HEY'S WAY

I remember when, at the beginning of his career with the Giants, Willie Mays couldn't buy a hit. The "Say Hey Kid" was shy and would get nervous if newspapermen came near his locker. He kind of kept to himself, and his mind was always on baseball.

He could be a fan, too, as I discovered many years later. I was sitting next to Joe DiMaggio at a Gold Glove Awards dinner in the Waldorf-Astoria, about 1993 or '94, when along comes Willie Mays. "Joe, would you sign this for me?" Mays asks, handing DiMaggio one of the baseballs given to attendees at the dinner. Here was one of the best ballplayers I'd ever seen asking the greatest ballplayer I'd ever seen for his autograph.

Joe thought for a while about what he was going to write—he wanted to come up with the proper sentiment for Willie. I forget exactly how DiMaggio phrased his message, but it was highly complimentary to Mays. Joe had a lot of respect for Willie Mays, but then, who didn't?

In September 1963, Casey warmed up the crowd for a return engagement by the former New York/now San Francisco Giant. A decade or so later, a player who always felt like part of the city's baseball family was back in New York, a member of the Mets.

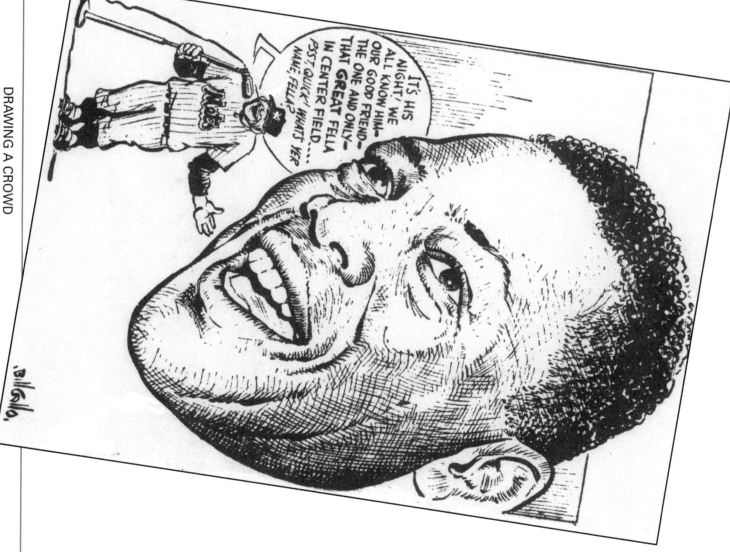

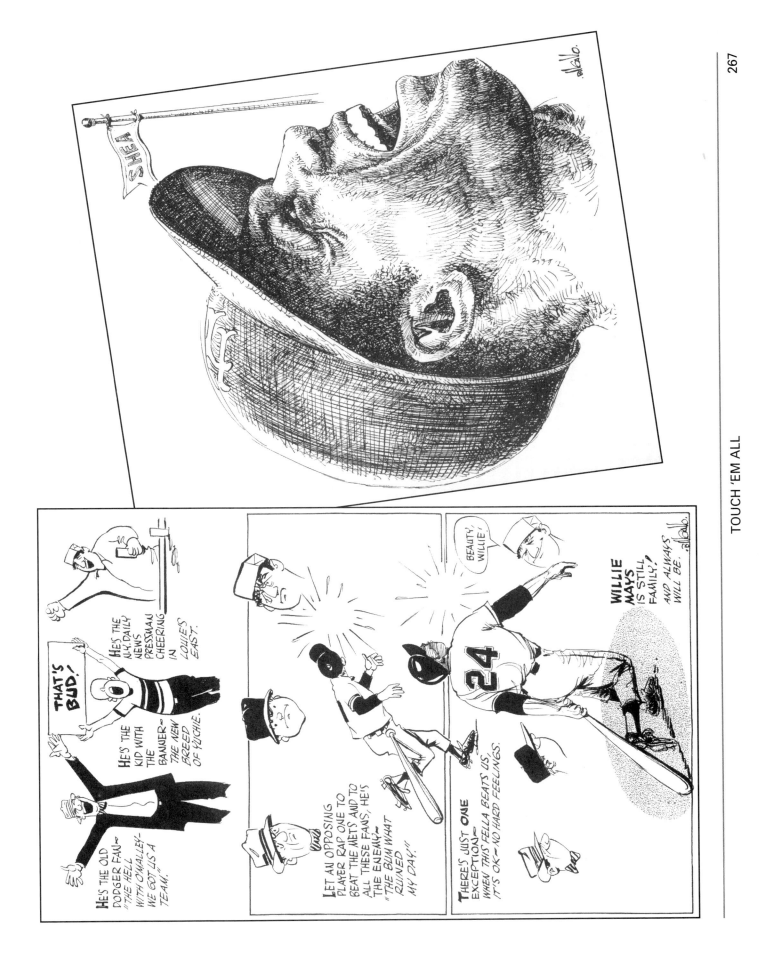

TOUCH 'EM ALL

THE MOON AND THE STARS

The Miracle Mets of 1969 were like a band building to a crescendo. That summer, I ran into several members of the team at a dinner in Washington to mark baseball's centennial. This was the time of the first lunar landing, so I asked them about their own prospects of reaching the heavens after years of losing records. Could they actually win the pennant? I was struck by how positive their responses were. It was then that I started to realize: "This could happen."

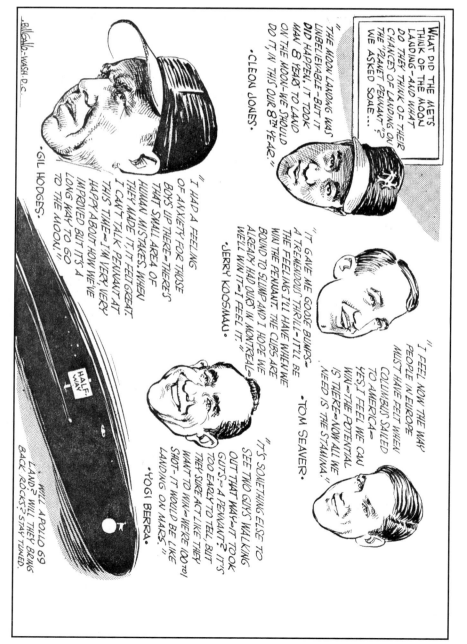

WHAT DID THE METS THINK OF THE MOON LANDING—AND WHAT DO THEY THINK OF THEIR CHANCES OF LANDING ON THE "PLANET PENNANT"? WE ASKED SOME...

"THE MOON LANDING WAS UNBELIEVABLE—BUT IT DID HAPPEN. IT TOOK MAN 8 YEARS TO LAND ON THE MOON—WE SHOULD DO IT, IN THIS OUR 8TH YEAR."
• CLEON JONES •

"IT GAVE ME GOOSE BUMPS— A TREMENDOUS THRILL—IT'LL BE THE FEELING I'LL HAVE WHEN WE WIN THE PENNANT. THE CUBS ARE BOUND TO SLUMP AND I HOPE WE ALREADY HAD OURS IN MONTREAL— WE'LL WIN IT—I FEEL IT."
• JERRY KOOSMAN •

"I FEEL NOW THE WAY PEOPLE IN EUROPE MUST HAVE FELT WHEN COLUMBUS SAILED TO AMERICA— YES, I FEEL WE CAN WIN—THE POTENTIAL IS THERE—NOW ALL WE NEED IS THE STAMINA."
• TOM SEAVER •

"IT'S SOMETHING ELSE TO SEE TWO GUYS WALKING OUT THAT WAY—IT TOOK GUTS—A PENNANT? IT'S TOO EARLY TO TELL, BUT THEY SURE ACT LIKE THEY WANT TO WIN—WE'RE 100 TO 1 SHOT—IT WOULD BE LIKE LANDING ON MARS."
• YOGI BERRA •

"I HAD A FEELING OF ANXIETY FOR THOSE BOYS UP THERE—THERE'S THAT SMALL AREA OF HUMAN MISTAKES. WHEN THEY MADE IT, IT FELT GREAT. I CAN'T TALK PENNANT AT THIS TIME—I'M VERY, VERY HAPPY ABOUT HOW WE'VE IMPROVED BUT IT'S A LONG WAY TO GO TO THE MOON."
• GIL HODGES •

HALF WAY

WILL APOLLO 69 LAND? WILL THEY BRING BACK ROCKS? STAY TUNED.

BillGallo—WASH. D.C.

THINKING BIG

During spring training, I saw signs that these young Mets might be shooting for bigger things that year. And as early as the first week of the season, people were starting to take stock of Mets center fielder Tommie Agee and his teammates.

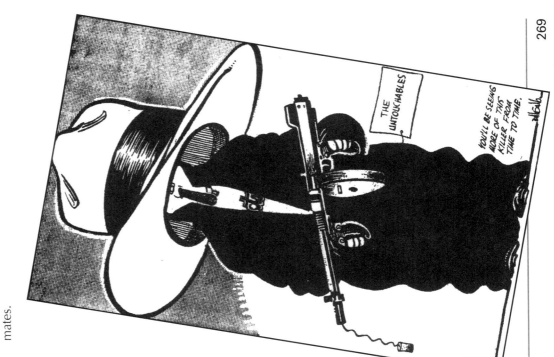

TOUCH 'EM ALL

A GIANT LEAP FOR MET-KIND

By the summer, fans were getting the idea that a Mets' pennant was not such a crazy idea. The team was stripping away its image as perennial losers, inspiring a naked takeoff on *Oh! Calcutta!* in the cartoon at far left.

Against the backdrop of the space program, the Mets completed their mission on October 16, 1969. The Mets were on top of the world and that put a broad smile on manager Gil Hodges (next page). The drawing was originally slated for Page One of *The News*, but deadlines got in the way and it ran inside.

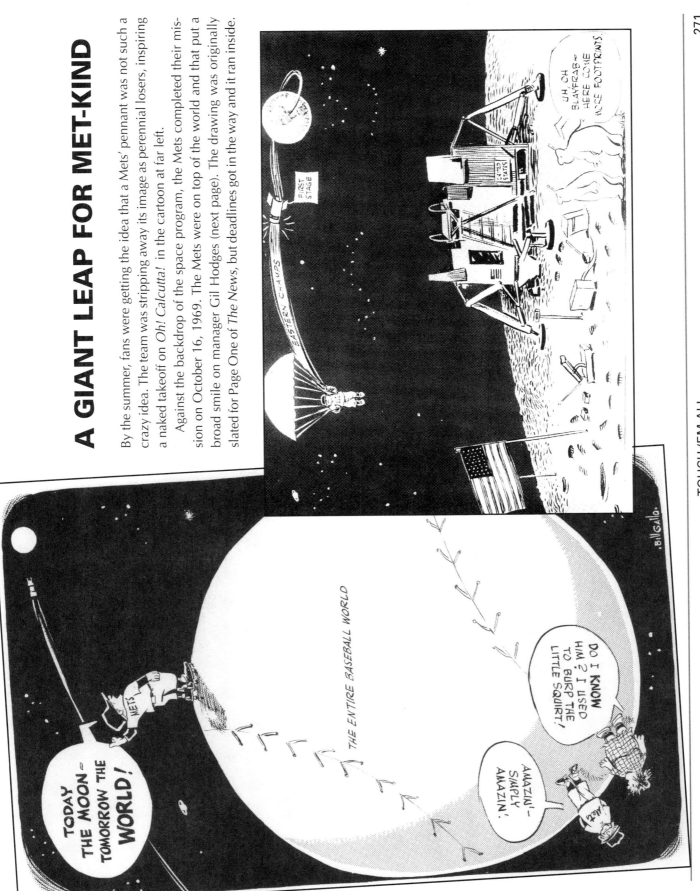

TOUCH 'EM ALL

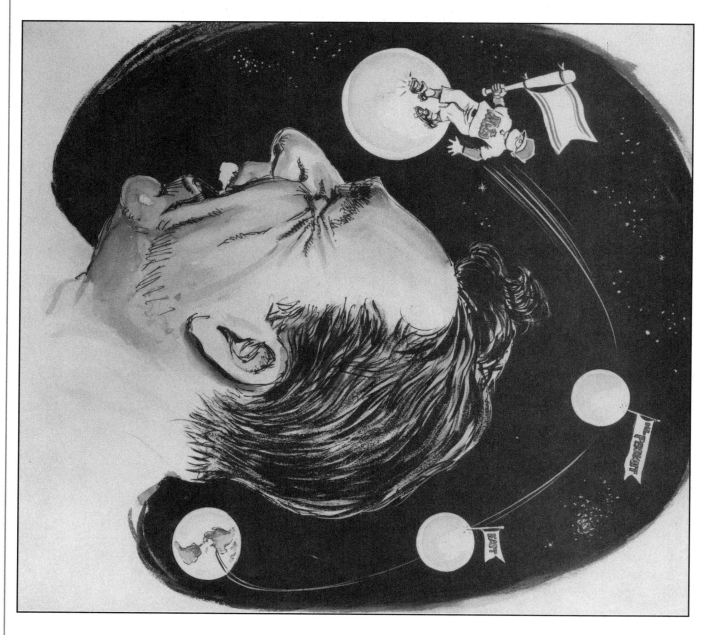

CHAPTER TWENTY-ONE

PAWS FOR EFFECT

A BIG PROBLEM

A cartoonist has to be dogged in his search for the right image, and that's where the animal kingdom can enter the picture. Former Cincinnati Reds owner Marge Schott, for example, would bring her pet Saint Bernard named Schottzie all around with her.

She also had a knack for saying the wrong thing—like finding something praiseworthy in Hitler—which would get her called on the carpet by baseball's ruling Executive Council. So I combined those two elements in this cartoon.

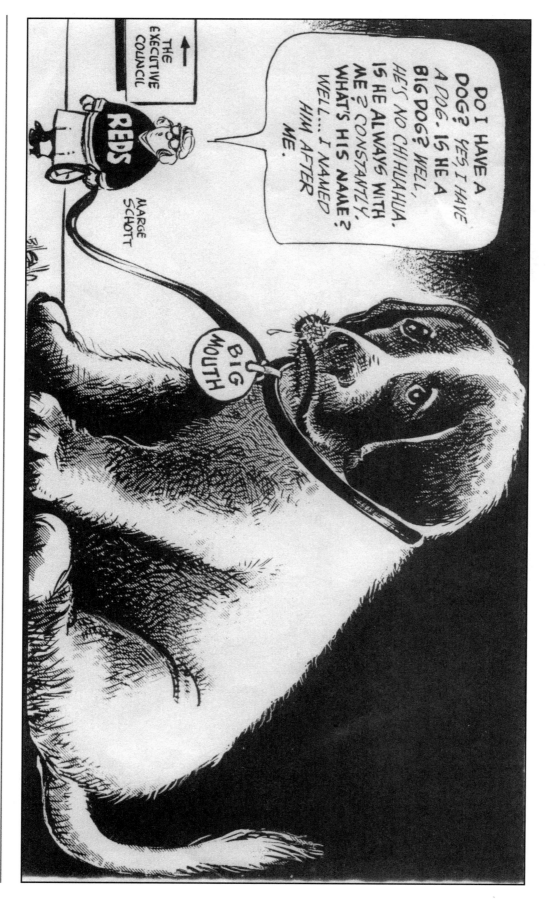

HORNS OF A DILEMMA

Curt Flood's problems were of a far different kind. In the days before free agency, he refused a trade from the Cardinals to the Phillies, challenging the system that bound a baseball player to one team indefinitely. He sat out the 1970 season, then quickly ended a comeback bid with the Senators the following year by buying a one-way ticket to Barcelona. The cartoon below, from April 1971, depicts Flood's struggle. Bullfighting also seemed to fit when I noted the elusive nature of a no-hitter in May 1967.

THE DESTINATION OF **CURT FLOOD** IS SAID TO BE SPAIN—WHERE HE WILL FIGHT THE BULL WE ALL FACE ON OCCASION IN OUR LIVES. BEFORE ANY KILL OF A BULL, COMES THE "FAENA DE CAPOTE"— THAT'S WHEN THE MATADOR USES HIS CAPE TO TEASE THE BEAST.

THROWING GOOSE EGGS

Players' nicknames are a natural source of ideas. Yankees reliever Rich "Goose" Gossage lent himself to this flight of fancy, while Orel Hershiser's moniker, The Bulldog, given to him by Dodgers manager Tommy Lasorda, added bite to a 1988 World Series illustration.

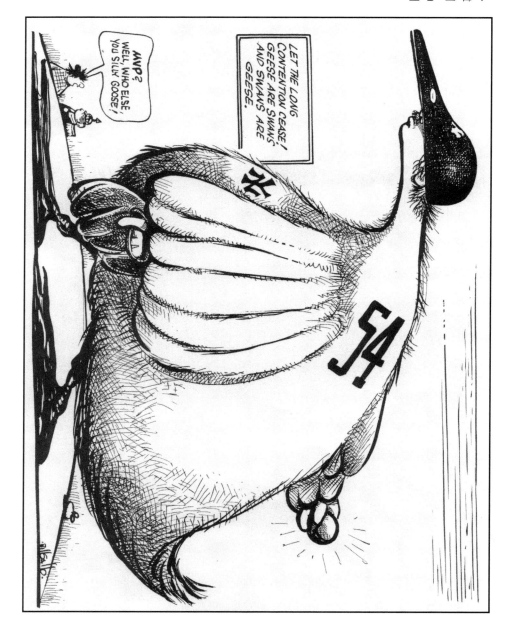

PAWS FOR EFFECT

WHALE OF A TALE

James Douglas, the heavyweight boxer who pulled off a huge upset over Mike Tyson in February 1990, is nicknamed Buster, but by the time he lost his crown to Evander Holyfield the following October, "Whale" seemed to better describe his shape. Barbs like that are hurled at famous athletes all the time. That's the price they pay for living in a fishbowl.

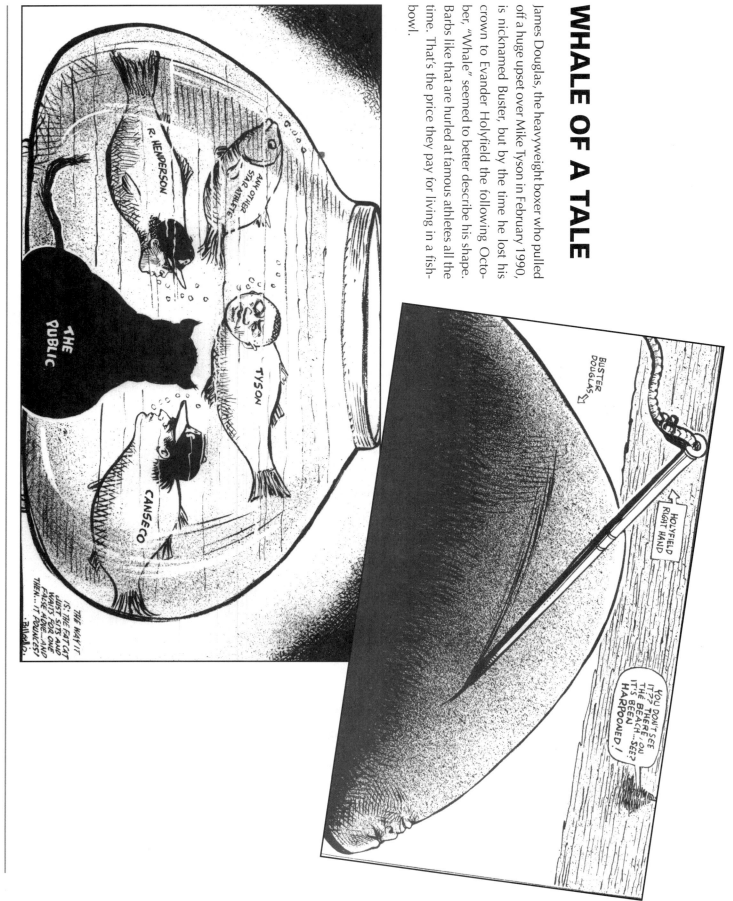

PURRING ALONG

John Vanbiesbrouck brought catlike reflexes to the Rangers' goaltending duties in the mid-'80s, and I used a tiger to embody them. Long Island University's basketball team, meanwhile, was on the opposite end of the food chain when in the hunt at the National Invitation Tournament in March 1968. Their nickname is The Blackbirds, but a mouse worked better in this setting.

PAWS FOR EFFECT

GOING TO THE DOGS

A rich woman's leashed dogs seemed to capture sports' subservience to TV money. The mutts in the dogfight drawing below expressed my fatigue with the sports labor wars.

PAWS FOR EFFECT

FITS THE BILL

The Mets of 1983 had a record of 68-94. The following season, with Rookie of the Year Dwight Gooden and new manager Davey Johnson, the team finished 90-72. Here's one way to summarize that striking turnaround.

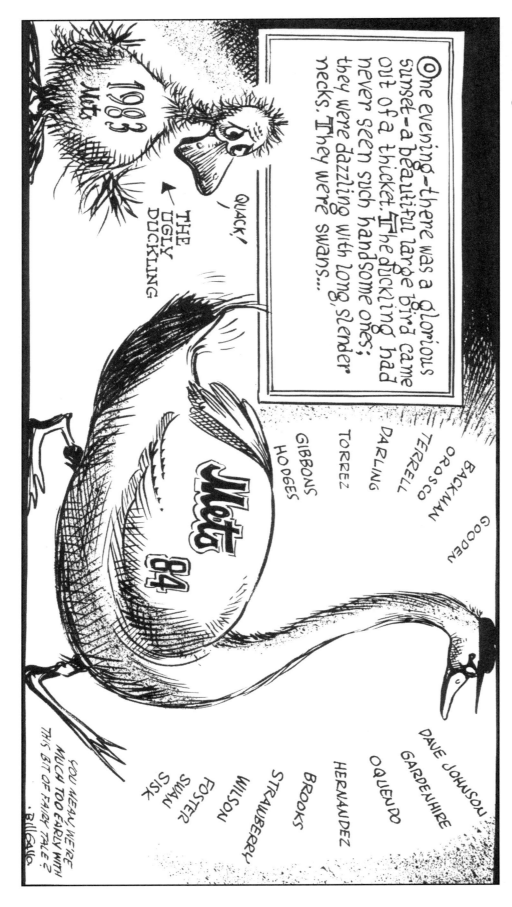

OH, DEER!

Olympic figure skaters Tonya Harding and Nancy Kerrigan had plenty of differences, and one of them was in their styles. I saw one as hard-charging on skates, the other as delicate.

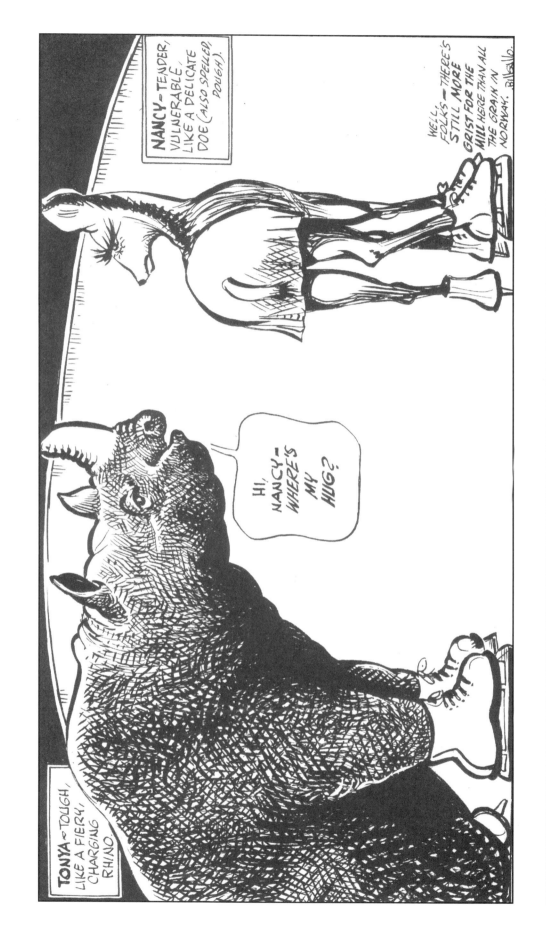

THE BIGGER THEY ARE . . .

To win the gold medal at the 1980 Olympics in Lake Placid, New York, the U.S. hockey team had to topple a hugely favored Soviet squad. The Americans pulled it off, though, and to convey the enormity of their upset, I searched for the biggest animal I could think of. A dinosaur did the job nicely. That prehistoric creature also symbolized the voracious appetite for money that has threatened sports.

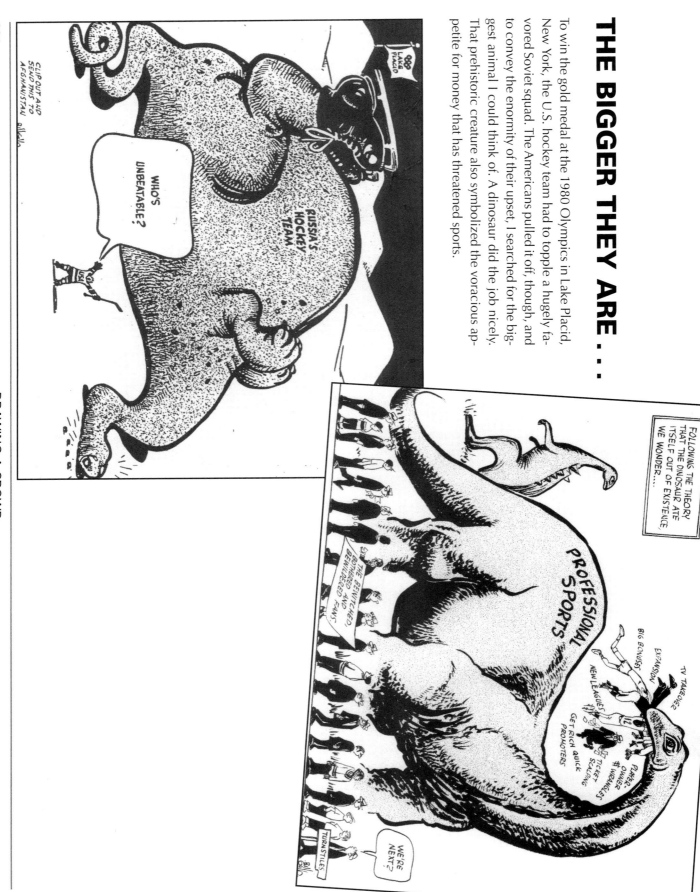

THE BRONX MOO

Phil Rizzuto was nicknamed The Scooter when he played shortstop for the Yankees, but it is his familiar broadcasting cry "Holy Cow!" that set up this cartoon.

IF I COULD TALK THROUGH THE ANIMALS

Seagulls don't normally harbor grudges against ballplayers, but Yankees outfielder Dave Winfield weren't too pleased either, and Winfield was actu-made their enemies list when a baseball he threw inadvertently killed one of the birds during a game

in Toronto in August 1983. The local authorities weren't too pleased either, and Winfield was actu-ally arrested. Still, there was room for some levity.

NEW LIFE FORMS

Sometimes, Mother Nature just can't provide the image that I need. So I put on the thinking cap and come up with something of my own. Take all the boxing organizations that have sprung up over the years—the WBA, WBC, IBF. They all have their own titles, and the result is that the heavyweight championship—once held by a single, recognizable individual—has been splintered and diminished. Four heads, though, aren't better than one.

THE SUM OF ITS PARTS

By building an imaginary athlete out of real ones, I've been able to single out qualities that have made sports stars great. Here I apply the approach to golf and to some Yankee legends.

A HEADS-UP IDEA

The gizmos I've invented over the years are like the characters that I've created; they help tell the story. The Telekeg, its patent still pending, has proven to be one of my most durable devices, and I've tapped it often over the years.

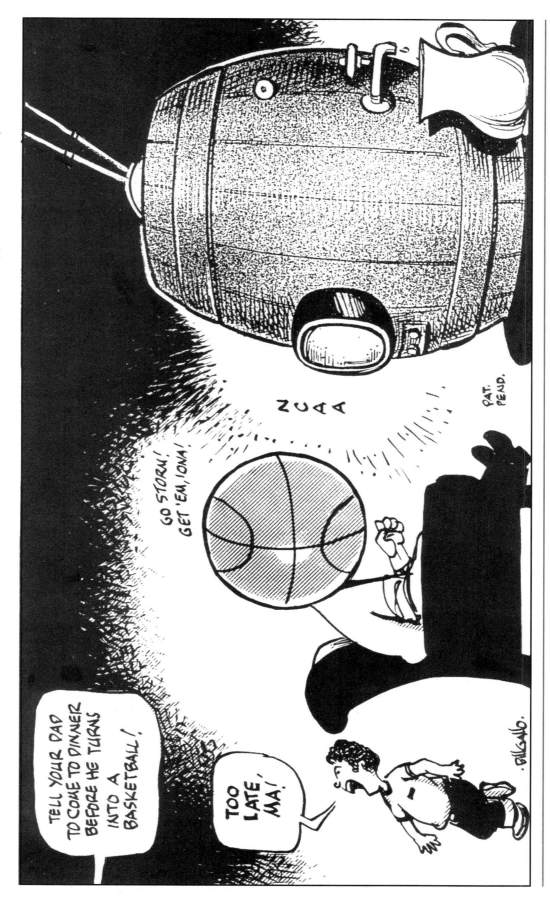

I AM A CAMERA

During the 1998 football season, when a blown call cost the Seattle Seahawks a game against the Jets, I proposed a portable referee-cam that spurred several name suggestions from fans. (One reader even built a small model of the device and mailed it to me.) I figure this kind of replay gadget was a more humane improvement over the camera-headed refs I had once envisioned.

PAWS FOR EFFECT

DOWN BY THE MILL STREAM

I like to call sports subjects "grist for my mill." Well, the mill really does exist and here's a chance to see it in action, from the 1999 baseball season.

CHAPTER TWENTY-TWO

MANAGING JUST FINE

TOP MANAGEMENT

There's something special about coaches—football coaches, baseball managers, boxing trainers. Bill Parcells, Joe Torre, Allie Sherman, they're all smart guys who could head a big company. Casey Stengel was smart, too, even if the world saw him as a humorous figure.

A manager has to have good players to succeed, just like a cabinetmaker has to have good tools. You can't build a cabinet with your bare hands.

But a successful manager adds something crucial, and it's not just a knowledge of the game. Plenty of guys have that. The real standouts are leaders who know how to win the respect of their players. There are different ways to do it—you don't have to be a drill instructor—but the bottom line is leadership.

Coaches and managers can leave their imprint on a team for the better, and three examples are the Jets' Bill Parcells, the Mets' Bobby Valentine and the Yankees' Joe Torre. Each improved his squad considerably soon after arriving.

BILL PARCELLS

BOBBY V

JOE T

AGE-OLD QUESTION: DOES THE MGR. (OR COACH) MAKE A MARKED DIFFERENCE IN HIS TEAM'S WON AND LOSS PERCENTAGE?

YES, NO QUESTION.

ABSOLUTELY.

"HEY, I COULDA TOLD YOU THAT!"

.BIGALIO.

LESSONS IN LIFE

Joe Lapchick, who coached St. John's basketball as well as the Knicks, was a dear friend, a great leader and a sensitive man. He was also a teacher. He wasn't aware that he was teaching, but he was—about life. He loved his players; he earned respect not through intimidation but with a velvet glove. He had a lot of faith in human nature.

Lou Carnesecca, one of Joe's prize pupils and a longtime assistant, became a top coach himself at St. John's. Here, I have Lapchick looking on during Lou's glory years in the 1980s, a time when players like Chris Mullin played for St. John's.

LEARNING AT HIS KNEE

In the 1970 NIT final, Carnesecca faced off against Marquette, coached by another Lapchick protégé, Al McGuire. I included a farewell to Lou because he was leaving St. John's to become general manager and coach of the ABA Nets. But like Lapchick, he would return from the pros for a second tour of duty at St. John's. Lapchick himself died later that year, at age seventy.

PARCELLS EXCELS

Bill Parcells is not exactly Vince Lombardi, but he's the closest I can think of. Like Lombardi, he's genuinely tough for a purpose—he wants to get the most out of his ball-players. He got a lot out of his Giants team during the Super Bowl season of 1986, a championship run I recounted in a portrait of the victorious coach.

Early in Bill's tenure with the Giants, I drew a cartoon in which I called him Chubby. He said to me, "You know, that was my father's nickname, Chubby. He was a coach, too." He didn't say it, but I got the sense that I might have offended him. Suddenly, my little joke didn't seem funny, but rather obvious, and I never did it again.

CURTAIN CALL

As he bowed out after his second Super Bowl title, early in 1991, I figured it was time for a glowing review. In January 1993, I borrowed from David Letterman in listing my reasons why Parcells would return to the coaching ranks, this time for the New England Patriots.

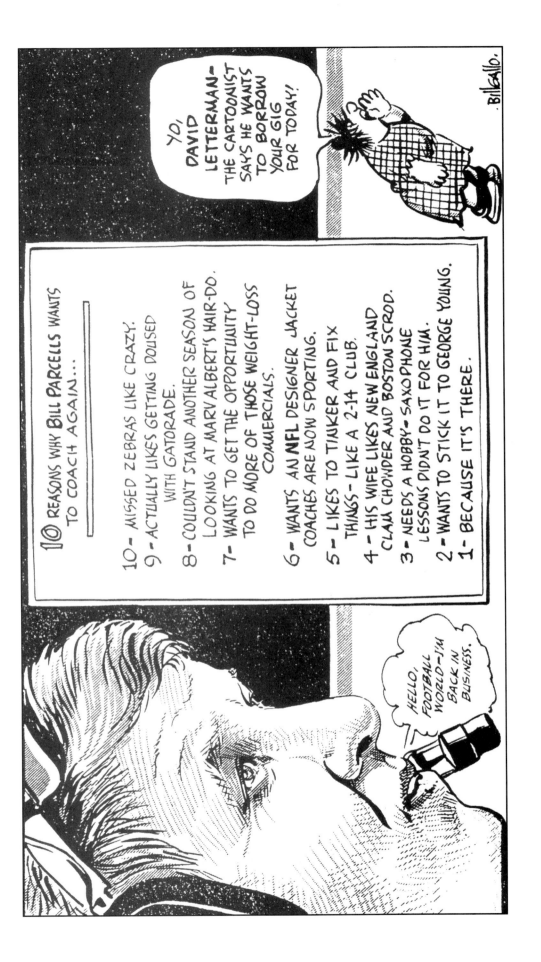

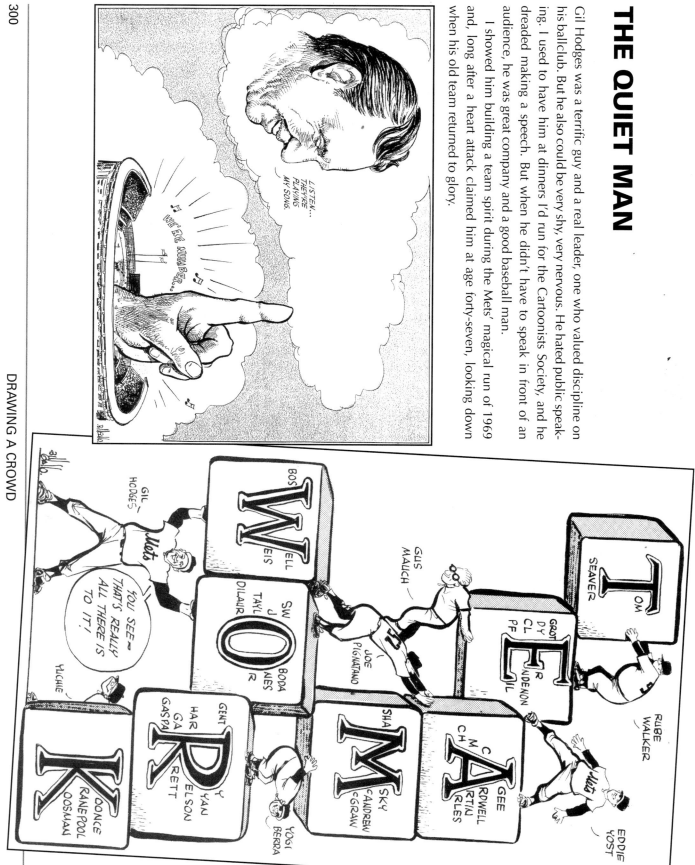

THE QUIET MAN

Gil Hodges was a terrific guy and a real leader, one who valued discipline on his ballclub. But he also could be very shy, very nervous. He hated public speaking. I used to have him at dinners I'd run for the Cartoonists Society, and he dreaded making a speech. But when he didn't have to speak in front of an audience, he was great company and a good baseball man.

I showed him building a team spirit during the Mets' magical run of 1969 and, long after a heart attack claimed him at age forty-seven, looking down when his old team returned to glory.

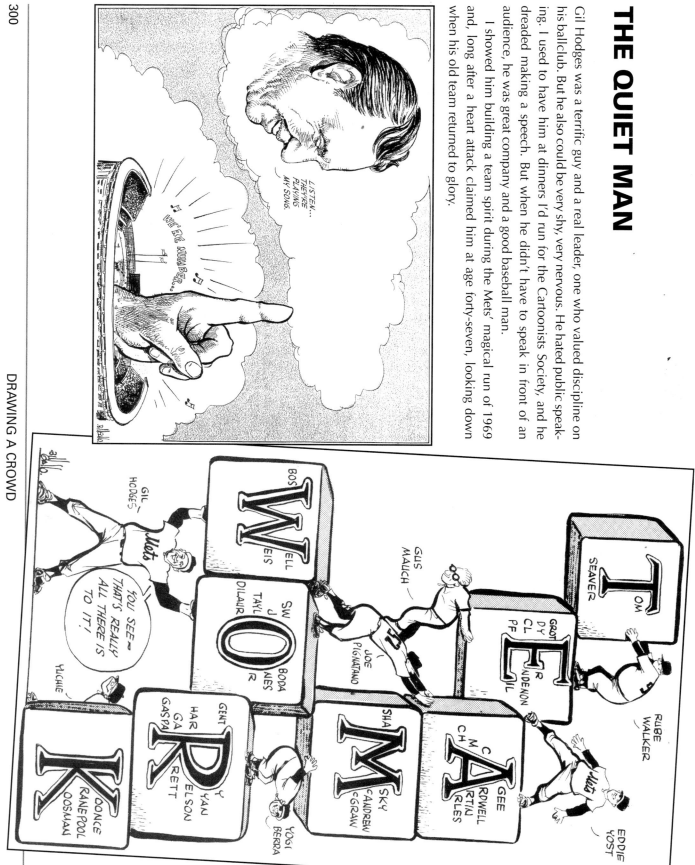

THE TORRE STORY

Joe Torre has a quiet, low-key kind of leadership. He doesn't present a tough-guy image, yet his players respect him. He's the strong silent type. Torre is also a textbook example of how you need the right tools to win. Before he came to the Yankees, he never made it to the World Series. His record was well below .500, and he had to face the music managing the Mets during their lean years of the late '70s and early '80s.

Given a team loaded with talent like the Yankees, he won a world championship in 1996, his first season in the Bronx. Joe then made it three titles in four years, including a 1998 squad that went 125-50.

JET PILOT

Weeb Ewbank was a great judge of talent, and one of his best discoveries was Johnny Unitas. With Joe Namath, the talent was evident beforehand, but Unitas's skills developed as he was coached. "He was a teacher more than a coach," Unitas recalled at Ewbank's funeral in November 1998. "He gave me my chance."

I had Casey greet Weeb upon his arrival with the Jets in 1963; it was the year in which the team changed its name from the Titans, so a link to the Mets seemed fitting. I saluted Ewbank upon his farewell as Jets coach a decade later.

THE FIVE FACES OF TOM

Tom Landry, longtime coach of the Dallas Cowboys, was proof that you don't have to be a screamer to be a successful leader. He was stone-faced on the sidelines, which made for a lighthearted cartoon after his Cowboys pulled out a playoff victory against the Atlanta Falcons in January 1981.

MANAGING JUST FINE

RALPH'S LAMENT

Ralph Houk, a cigar-puffing former Army Ranger major, had a tough-guy reputation. When he first arrived to manage the Yankees in 1961, the team was still reeling off pennants, but during a subsequent tour of duty with the Yanks, a mediocre lineup had Houk singing the blues, or at least a recast version of "Mrs. Robinson." The original of the cartoon at right hangs in Gallagher's Steak House on Manhattan's West 52nd Street.

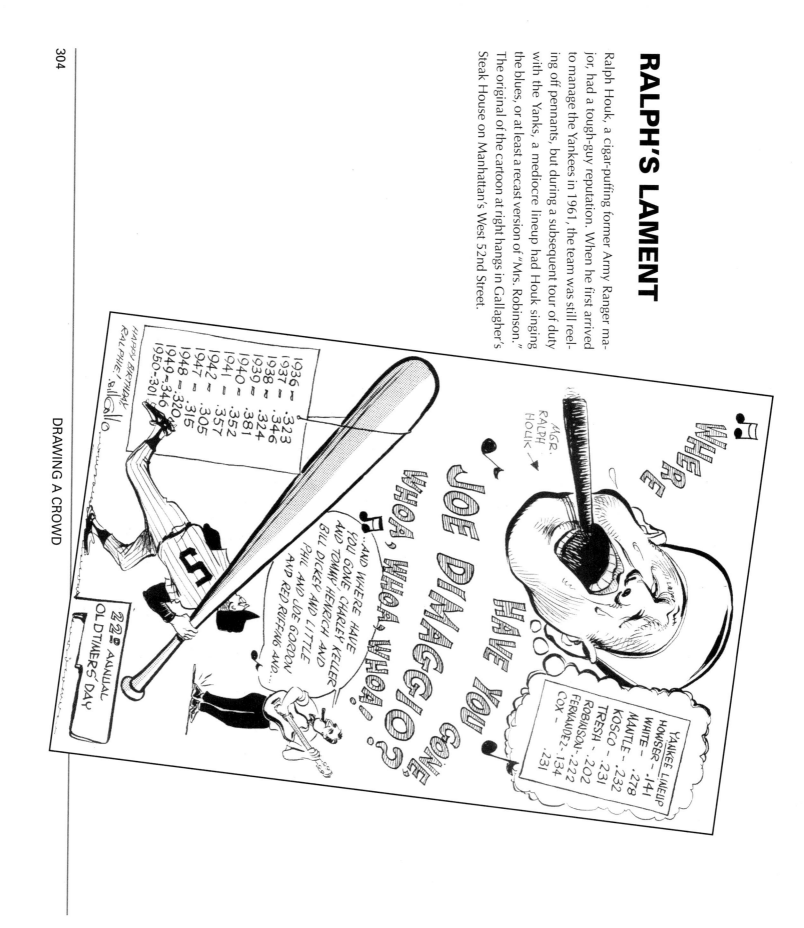

MY FUNNY VALENTINE

Tossed from a game during the 1999 season, Mets manager Bobby Valentine responded with a put-on: He put on a disguise in an attempt to stay in the dugout. I took that idea a step further.

AT A LOSS

You have to respect the football coach. The team plays only sixteen games a year in the pros, and you have to win most of them. Those that don't have to face hostile crowds and the prospect of their own imminent demise. The Jets' futility reached its peak in the mid-'90s regime of Rich Kotite, who seemed always to be operating under a cloud, while the Giants had gone through a series of coaches during their drought in the late 1960s and the 1970s.

MANAGING JUST FINE

MAKING A SPLASH

When football players took to dumping Gatorade on their coaches to celebrate a big victory, I wondered how the old-school coaches would react. I don't think Lombardi would have reacted well, but then again, it was a sign of a changing society. I'm not saying that's good or bad—just different.

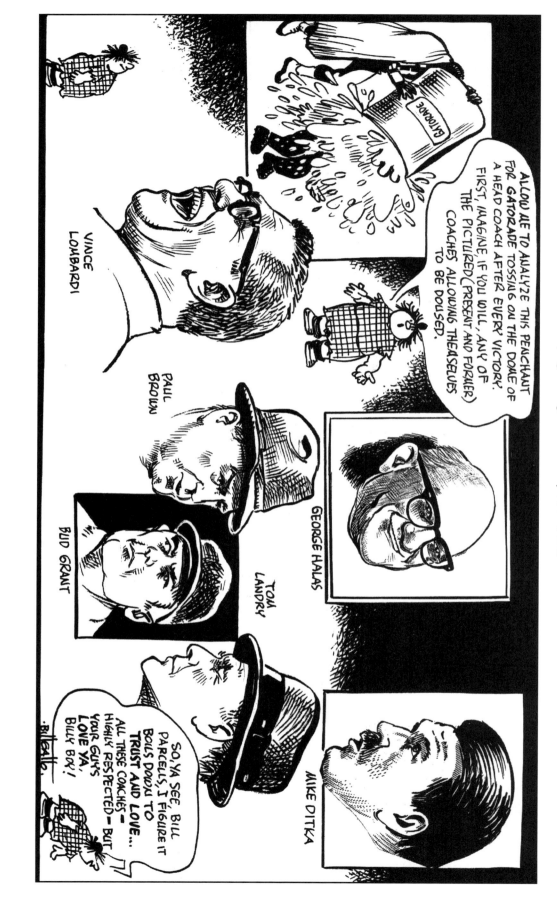

CHAPTER TWENTY-THREE

THE POLITICAL ARENA

STOP THE WORLD

I admire a lot of editorial cartoonists. I look at their drawings and try to imagine how I would approach those same subjects. It's become popular to treat everything with humor, but that gets to be almost slapstick, and it demeans an artist's voice. I prefer poignancy.

I like editorial cartoonists such as Jeff MacNelly, Pat Oliphant, David Low, the great Herbert L. Block (better known as Herblock), the *Daily News'* Bill Schor and one of Schor's predecessors at *The News,* the Pulitzer Prize-winning C. D. Batchelor. Their work is direct and intelligent. I don't care which side the artist is on, but his work has to be intelligent. In fact it's almost better to disagree with the cartoonist, because he or she is getting you to think and to debate. That kind of reaction is the mark of an outstanding political cartoonist.

I favored the direct approach in my reaction to Robert F. Kennedy's assassination in June 1968, as he pursued the presidency. Two days before the shooting, I had included the New York senator in a drawing about the Belmont Stakes, which had been won in an upset by Stage Door Johnny. After Kennedy's murder, the world seemed to be going mad, and a straitjacket was the logical remedy.

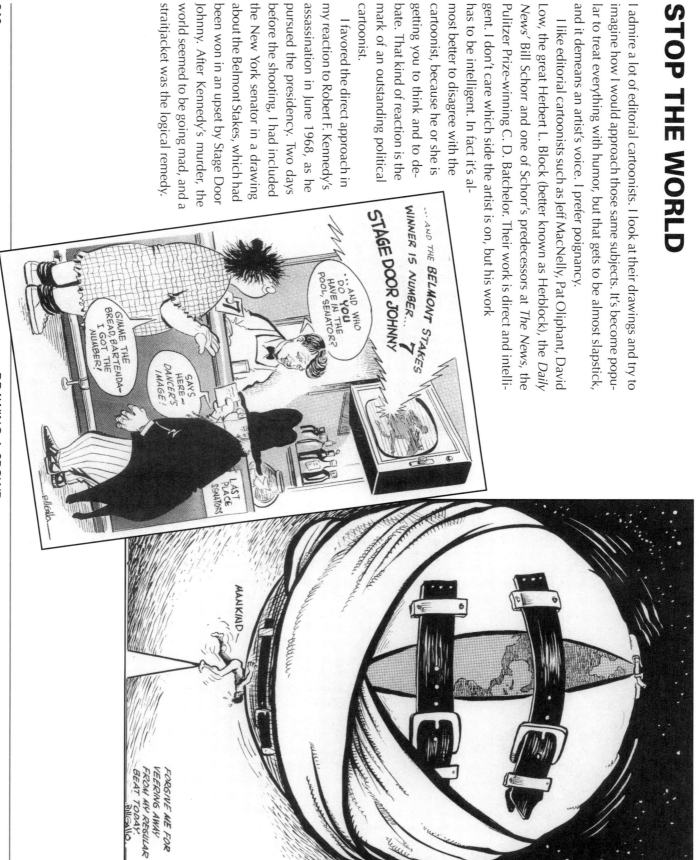

CALLING THE SIGNALS

Richard Nixon was once billed as the nation's No. 1 football fan, but even the president of the United States couldn't get NFL commissioner Pete Rozelle to lift the television blackout on playoff games in the home team's city. The impasse did get the Chief Executive into one of my cartoons in December 1972.

IT'S ALL IN THE GAME

Nixon wasn't just an armchair quarterback. He went so far as to suggest a play to coach George Allen of the Washington Redskins, which I joked about in an illustration that also cast foreign affairs expert Henry Kissinger in an off-panel role. Later, Henry showed up as a possible peacemaker when football players and team owners lined up against one another during a time of labor unrest.

SERVING A POINT

"Ping-Pong diplomacy" became a tool of international relations in the spring of 1971 as a U.S. table-tennis team traveled to communist China. This brought out the idealist in Basement Bertha, as I put my own topspin on events.

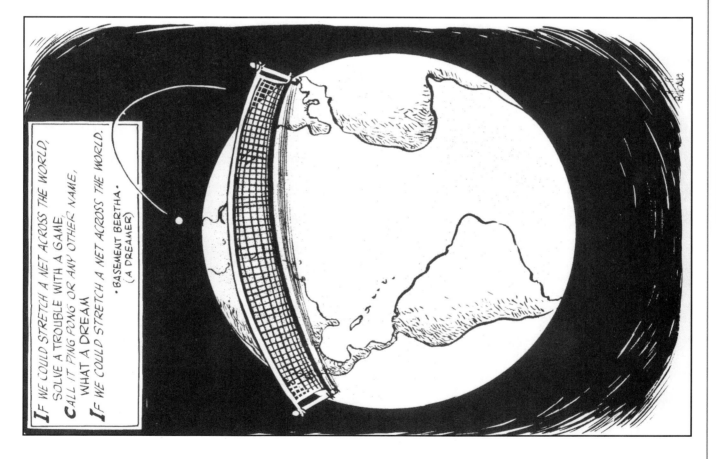

IF WE COULD STRETCH A NET ACROSS THE WORLD,
SOLVE A TROUBLE WITH A GAME,
CALL IT PING PONG OR ANY OTHER NAME,
WHAT A DREAM.
IF WE COULD STRETCH A NET ACROSS THE WORLD.

• BASEMENT BERTHA •
(A DREAMER)

. . . A TIME FOR PEACE

The Vietnam War officially ended for the United States at 7:00 P.M. on January 27, 1973—at least that was when the peace treaty signed in Paris took effect. After a decade or so of combat and death, protest and national division, it was time for the last word on the subject. That word, inscribed on my drawing board in the following day's illustration, stood in simple contrast to all the death and destruction that had preceded it.

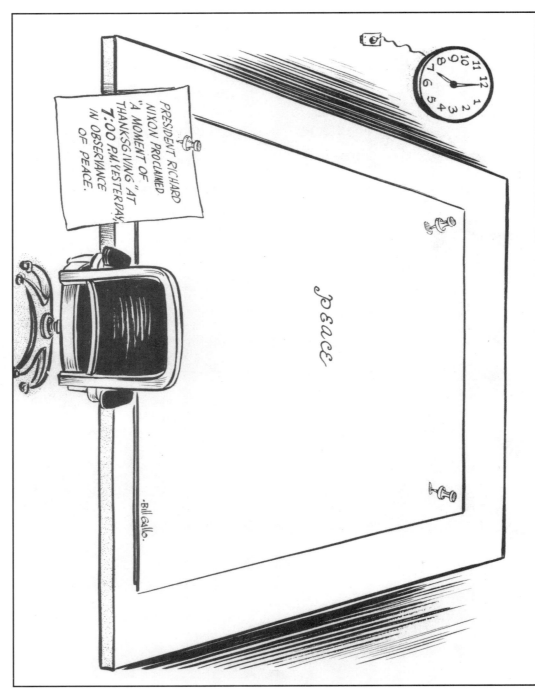

SUBSTITUTION

President Gerald Ford knew something about football himself (he once played center for the University of Michigan), so I gave him good field position on the White House lawn when he succeeded Richard Nixon in the wake of Watergate.

THE POLITICAL ARENA

THE STATE OF SPORTS

It's not a national issue, but the relocation of New York teams to New Jersey—even the threat of it—has been a source of regional friction going back at least to the '70s. In February 1977, the Jets had run out of patience with their lack of access to Shea Stadium during baseball season, and the gridders were threatening to cross the Hudson as the Giants had done. (It didn't happen in '77, but Jets owner Leon Hess did eventually transfer the team to the Meadowlands in 1984.) I found some familiar images to tell the story.

WING FORMATION

It's not easy to top the pregame hype of the Super Bowl, but Bertha and I put everything aside to greet the hostages returning from Iran in January 1981. Next to the stark image of the bare-limbed tree (complete with hostage ribbon), the cloud provided a buoyant backdrop for the plane's arrival. An artist always has to think about composition.

THE POLITICAL ARENA

SOLDIERING ON

A desert scene from the Gulf War of 1991 helped put the escalating baseball salaries in perspective.

STRANGE BEDFELLOWS

The Monica Lewinsky scandal of 1998 gave Bertha an opportunity to quiz past U.S. presidents about affairs of state. Got a lot of mail on this one—most of it positive.

THE QUESTION
—BY BILL GALLO

THIS, OF COURSE, IS FICTION—BUT WHAT WE'VE DONE HERE IS TO ASSIGN BERTHA TO ASK FORMER PRESIDENTS: "HAVE YOU EVER HAD AN AFFAIR?"

HEREWITH, USING A BIT OF WHIMSY, IS WHAT THEY MIGHT HAVE ANSWERED:

GEORGE, YOU'RE FIRST!

GEORGE WASHINGTON
"NOW, DON'T GO BELIEVING ALL THOSE LIES SAYING, I SLEPT HERE... I SLEPT THERE..."

ABE LINCOLN
"FOUR SCORE AND..."

WOODROW WILSON
"YOU WANT TO START WW II?"

JOHN F. KENNEDY
"NEVER! BUT, WHAT ARE YOU DOING AFTER THE SHOW, BABE?"

WILLIAM H. HARRISON
"LISTEN, I WAS IN OFFICE ONLY 32 DAYS."

WILLIAM H. TAFT
"NEXT QUESTION."

DWIGHT D. EISENHOWER
"GENERALLY SPEAKING, NO."

JAMES MONROE
"NO, IT WAS NOT IN MY DOCTRINE."

TEDDY ROOSEVELT
"YOU GOT THE RIGHT TEDDY?"

HARRY S. TRUMAN
"ALWAYS STAYED OUT OF THE KITCHEN."

THOMAS JEFFERSON
"I'LL JUST TELL YOU THAT I WAS A WIDOWER FOR 43 YEARS."

ULYSSES S. GRANT
"I'D RATHER HAVE A DRINK."

FRANKLIN D. ROOSEVELT
"AH, YES—THOSE FIRESIDE CHATS..."

THE POLITICAL ARENA

319

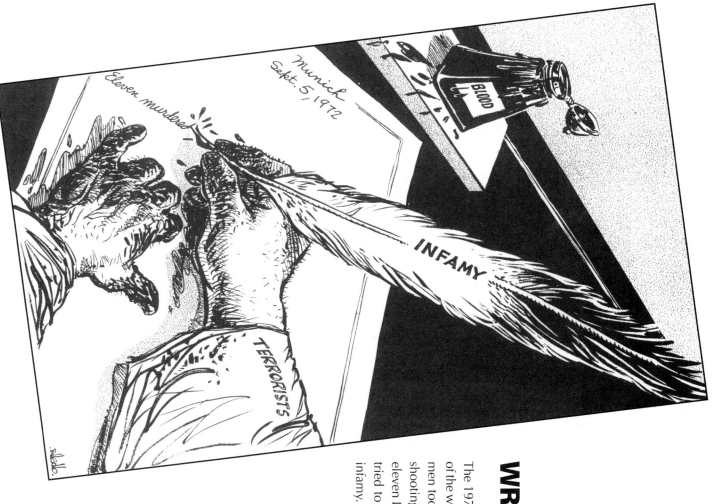

WRITTEN IN BLOOD

The 1972 Munich Olympics was the scene of one of the worst tragedies in sports history, as Arab gunmen took Israeli athletes hostage. By the time the shooting stopped, the terrorists had the blood of eleven Israelis on their hands. With this drawing, I tried to inscribe that slaughter into the annals of infamy.

CHAPTER TWENTY-FOUR

ALI AND JOE D

PORTRAIT ON CANVAS

Muhammad Ali has injected so much drama into our lives. Ali kept evolving, kept getting better in every sense, and my view of him evolved as well.

There was a time when I thought Ali was a braggart, and I drew him as perpetually talking. I wasn't used to that kind of self-serving behavior from a pro athlete. Then I realized it was all an act to boost the gate, and I found him to be a genius at it. He was a tremendous salesman, and the product was himself. He knew people would pay for the chance to see him get beat. He was having fun, and it worked. It played to his self-confidence.

Eventually, I came to see the kind of guy he really was: honest, forthright, someone who cared about his fellow man, black or white. He's still that way. And he showed us a lot about courage during the Vietnam War. He was so sure of himself that he was willing to go to jail for his principles.

The image at right was drawn in a pen-and-ink sketch style that I like to use on occasion, particularly when I want to emphasize the subject rather than the idea. I feel my way through a drawing like this, with the goal being a more realistic portrait.

GOING THE DISTANCE

The first time I met Ali was in 1962—between numbers three and four in this bio of him I drew in 1979. There was no "Ali" then; he was Cassius Clay. He had registered a series of knockouts in 1961, and he had come to New York to fight Sonny Banks, whom he stopped in the fourth round.

News colleague Dick Young and I were at a boxing dinner at the Hotel Commodore, now the Grand Hyatt. Dick, Ali and I—just the three of us—were sitting around a small table, and we talked for about an hour. What impressed Dick and me was Ali's intelligence, the way he could express himself. We got to talking about life ever after, and he said, "What do think is going to happen? Where are you going to go when you're in that little box in that little hole? You're going no place."

ALI AND JOE D

ONE MOORE TIME

Towards the end of '62, I jabbed at Ali's boastfulness before he took on Archie Moore, whom I nicknamed "Long Pants" from the length of his boxing shorts. Ali made good on his word and put away the former light-heavyweight champ, then in his late forties, in four rounds.

DIDN'T SEE IT COMING

On February 25, 1964, I sat in a Manhattan movie house expecting to see a good feature attraction, although the ending seemed predictable. Broadcast live from Miami via closed-circuit television, the heavyweight title bout pit twenty-two-year-old challenger Muhammad Ali (then Cassius Clay) against the champ, Sonny Liston, a mean old SOB who was probably at the top of his game. Ali was a big underdog, and the consensus was that Liston would silence "The Louisville Lip." I also figured that the challenger would spend most of his time in the ring ducking Sonny's punches.

As soon as I saw Liston and Ali together, I got a surprise: Liston, whom I regarded as this big, powerful man, was the smaller of the two boxers! Still, I didn't think Ali was going to beat him; I just didn't see him as champion.

Then they fought, and I could not believe what I was seeing. Ali was clearly superior. He had too much speed for Liston, who sat on his stool—his face puffed, his eyes cut—and threw in the towel before the seventh round.

ALI AND JOE D

HAND ME THE ERASER

As a rule, I stand by my work, particularly the opinions I express in them. But there's an exception to every rule, and this drawing is one. I was saying that Ali was using religion to evade the draft, but I would come to regret that sentiment. This is one cartoon I wish I could have back.

BIG SALE!
CLERICAL GARB!
REASONABLY PRICED!

128
DRAFT BOARD
LOCAL BIG

—Billcolo.

BEHIND THE SCENES

Ali was fortunate to have in his corner a great trainer, Angelo Dundee. They were together for eighteen years, with never a cross word between them, and afterward remained the best of friends.

But Ali himself knew what to do and was a very hard worker, despite all his bantering with the press. Muhammad would urge on his sparring partners to hit him, tell them, "Come on, come on." And when they weren't laying enough leather on him, he'd chase them away and get someone else in there. Ali trained his body to take these blows—and he could take a punch better than any heavyweight who ever lived. In 1972, I sketched him at his training camp in Deer Lake, Pennsylvania.

ALI AND JOE D

WHEN YOU'RE SMILING . . .

Muhammad got a big kick out of putting on newspapermen. A bunch of us took a memorable bus ride with him before the title fight he gave to Floyd Patterson in 1965. We all went with Ali to the Catskills training camp of Patterson, whom Muhammad had nicknamed The Rabbit. For good measure, he brought along a bag of carrots. "For the Rabbit," he informed us.

We had more fun going up to that place on the bus. Ali was telling jokes and laughing. As we neared the end of our journey, the champ insisted on driving the bus himself. He didn't go a hundred yards when he put that bus in a ditch. We had to walk the rest of the way, and Ali laughed at us the whole time, because for him this was just more road work.

When we got there, he made a big fuss out of giving those carrots to Floyd, spreading them around the apron of the ring.

Ali could always make you smile. I tried to do the same with this 1975 drawing of him facing one of his toughest opponents, his soon-to-be ex-wife Belinda.

FIGHTS, ACTION, CAMERA

In 1977, Ali's life story was told onscreen, so I took a turn as a movie reviewer, giving *News* critic Kathleen Carroll the day off.

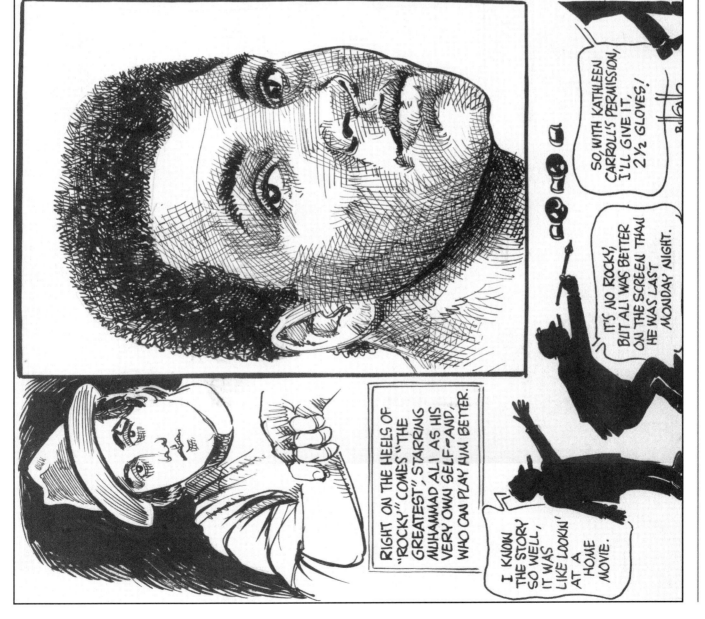

ALI AND JOE D

RETURN TO SPLENDOR

Ali fought twice in 1974, and together those bouts put him back on top. In January, again at Madison Square Garden, he avenged his loss to Joe Frazier and also put to rest the notion that his career was over. In fact, his finest hour came that October in Zaire, as Ali wore out George Foreman with his "rope-a-dope" strategy and then knocked him out to regain his crown. He also silenced the skeptics, including yours truly. My News colleague Phil Pepe, though, had called it right—Ali by a knockout. He accurately observed beforehand: "A cloak of invincibility has been draped around George Foreman, and I'm not convinced it is deserved."

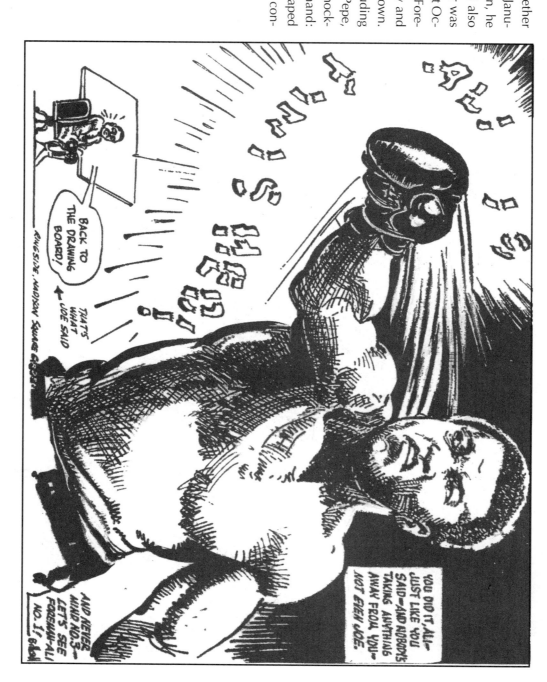

ALI AND JOE D

KING OF THE '70S

Ali would fight Frazier one more time: the "Thrilla in Manilla," in September 1975. The champ stopped Joe in his tracks, but it took fourteen rounds and a monumental effort to do so.

Ali started the '70s returning from exile, and he ended them regaining his title for a third time and being declared athlete of the decade by the sports staff of *The News*. "He didn't just rule boxing," *The News* observed. "He was boxing."

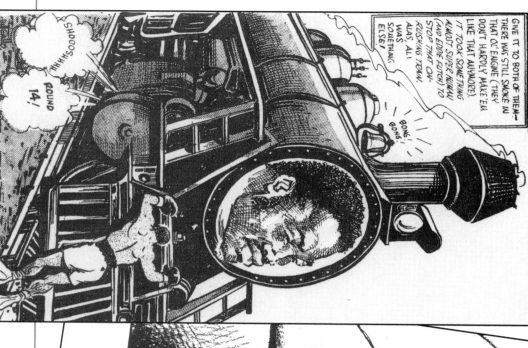

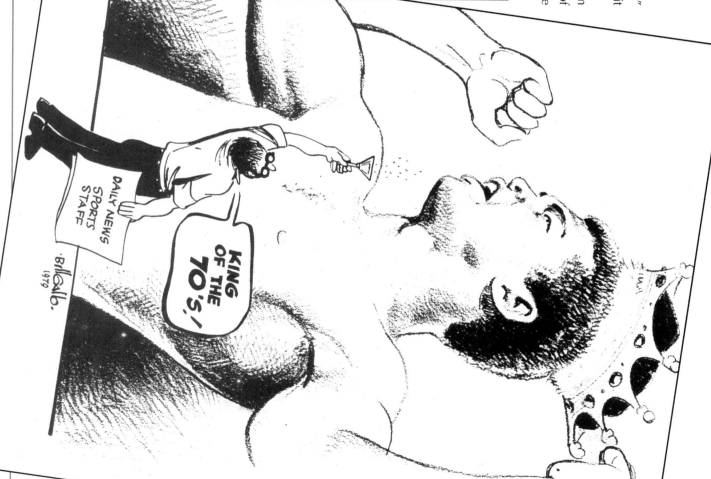

WINNER AND STILL CHAMP

Ali is a little slower these days, but he also has a look of contentment. I've seen women of all ages hug him and kiss his cheek—the kisses of mothers for their sons, aunts for their nephews. I've seen even tough old guys plant kisses on him. Ali, in turn, seems to love the sense of warmth he inspires.

And he can still charm. My wife and I attended a party along with him and his wife, Lonnie, when

Ali leaned over and gave my wife a kiss on the cheek.

"You like the girls, huh?" my wife responded. He leaned over and whispered in her ear: "What man don't?"

In December 1990, Muhammad used his world-wide celebrity to gain the release of Americans being held captive in Iraq—and posed a striking contrast with the dethroned champ Mike Tyson.

ALI AND JOE D

DELIVERING
THE PAUNCHLINE

At a sports dinner in September 1992, Ali and I sat next to each other. I did a quick sketch of him for old times' sake; he laughed and responded with a signature.

At the start of his career, Ali was not taken seriously by boxing purists. I watched this man evolve into one of the great champions and an equally fine human being, designated Sportsman of the Century in 1999. I'm proud to have known him.

LOTS OF HITS, A LONG RUN, NO ERRORS

When I think of Joe DiMaggio, I recall nothing but pleasant hours spent chatting about sports over lunch. Sometimes he would call me just to say hello or to talk about the Yankees or an upcoming boxing match; the fights were a longtime interest of his.

While I was in Joe's company, I was never in awe, because he wouldn't let you feel that way. He liked being with you as much as you liked being with him. There was no star business. Joe knew he was famous, but on the street he seemed genuinely surprised when someone stopped him and asked for an autograph. I suppose other people may have had a different experience with DiMaggio, but I never saw him turn down a request for his signature—and I was with him a lot.

Once we were heading to a restaurant when Joe was spotted by a group of Con Ed workers on the job. They applauded him like they would give an ovation to someone onstage. Joe was so flattered, he stopped and went over to them, shook everybody's hand and gave them all autographs.

ALI AND JOE D

A VISIT FROM THE CLIPPER

I struck up a friendship with Joe in the 1960s. The baseball writers used to put a show on at the Waldorf-Astoria; we'd do skits to lampoon the owners and the players. Sometimes the ballplayers, or former ballplayers, would be in the skits themselves, and DiMag happened to be in one. I got to know him during rehearsals, and we kind of hit it off.

To be a friend of this intensely private man, you had to obey a simple ground rule: leave his personal life alone, particularly the part concerning Marilyn Monroe. I respected that privacy and just talked sports with him. Oh sure, I considered asking something to see if he would drop his guard with me, but I never did. I figured I'd rather have

lunch with the guy and be his friend. Why ruin that just so I could find out how he treated Marilyn Monroe?

Even in his later years, Joe would drop by *The News* to visit, as I recorded in this illustration.

TOPS IN HIS FIELD

DiMag was quiet and reserved, but he could tell a story with wit and charm. We'd talk for hours about the game of baseball. I asked him once about his favorite baseball movie, and surprisingly it was not *Pride of the Yankees*, about his old teammate Lou Gehrig, but *Field of Dreams*. "I watched that movie every time it came on TV," he said. "[Kevin] Costner did a hell of a job. It was a fantasy with all the old names in there, and I love baseball history."

Of course, Joe made some history himself with that 56-game hitting streak in 1941. Here's how I recalled that accomplishment on its golden anniversary.

ALI AND JOE D

A MARK OF DISTINCTION

There were occasional runs at DiMaggio's hitting record in the decades since, Pete Rose's 44-game streak in 1978 being the most prominent. But Joe seldom had cause for concern, even though he told me on many occasions that he expected his mark to eventually be broken.

This drawing is from August 1987, when the Brewers' Paul Molitor was putting together a hitting streak of his own. He didn't get past 39 games, though.

SUMMER OF '41

DiMaggio was the MVP in 1941, even though Ted Williams hit .406 that year. Joe deserved it, too. Other people have hit .400, but nobody else has ever hit in 56 games in a row. Williams was the better hitter of the two, but DiMaggio was the better over-all ballplayer.

They say that long-ball hitters strike out a lot. Ruth and Mantle did, but DiMaggio rarely struck out. The same for Williams. As Casey Stengel might have observed, that was the advantage of standing sideways at home plate.

ALI AND JOE D

HE MADE IT LOOK EASY

DiMaggio had a presence, an aura, a dignity about him—in his face and in his movements. On and off the ballfield, he went about his business in an easy fashion. That's the beautiful part of genius: you make it look easy. Joltin' Joe was the epitome of that.

At the same time, he played as a perfectionist. Yogi Berra, renowned for being a man of many clever words, put it most succinctly about Joe: "I've never seen him make a mistake on the ballfield." That says a lot.

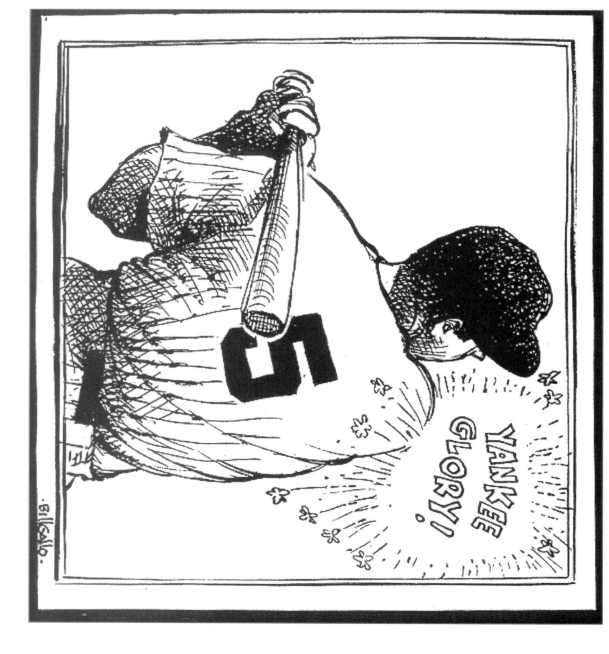

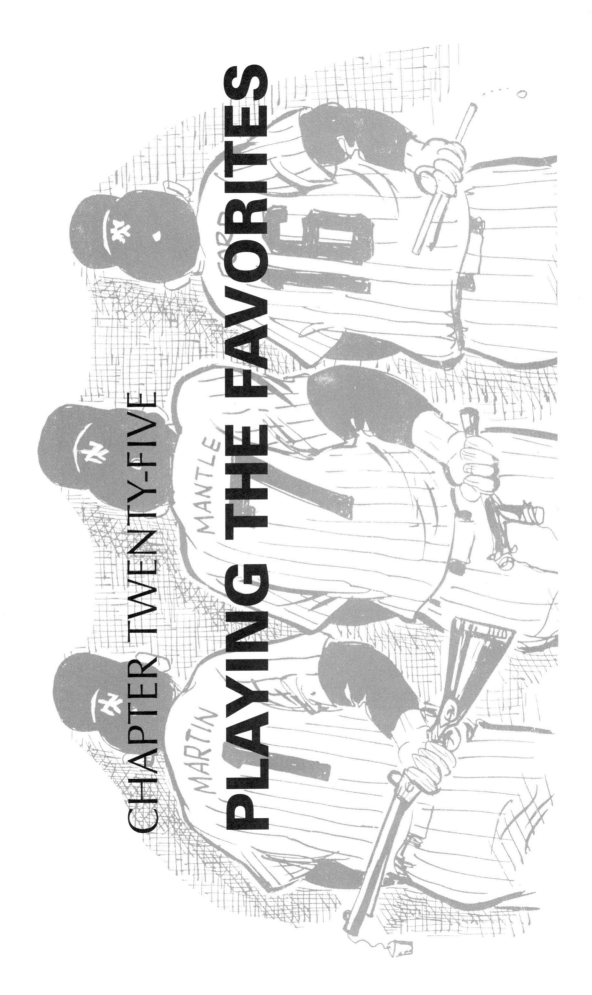

CHAPTER TWENTY-FIVE

PLAYING THE FAVORITES

HAVE FAITH
IN YOUR TEAM

Just as an athlete or fan likes to look back on the highlights of a game or a season, cartoonists enjoy recalling their favorite creations—at least this one does.

The NCAA basketball championship in 1985 came down to Georgetown and Villanova, two Catholic universities, although of different orders. My question is: Which team did the Pope root for?

IT'S SHOWTIME

Georgetown's John Thompson and St. John's Lou Carnesecca have been two of college basketball's best coaches, and in 1985 they met in the Final Four of the NCAA tourney (with Georgetown the victor). Both had a bounce in their step while in this national spotlight.

AT A LOSS

I take my sketch pad with me all over, and while in Spain in 1992 I caught this soccer player in the throes of anguish after a tough loss. Defeat has its sting in any language.

FLOATING AN IDEA

The bicentennial year of 1976 found the Yankees on the way to their first pennant in twelve years; the Mets about to enter a long dry spell. The team's opposite fates were reflected in Bertha's tub, as was the arrival of the tall ships in New York Harbor.

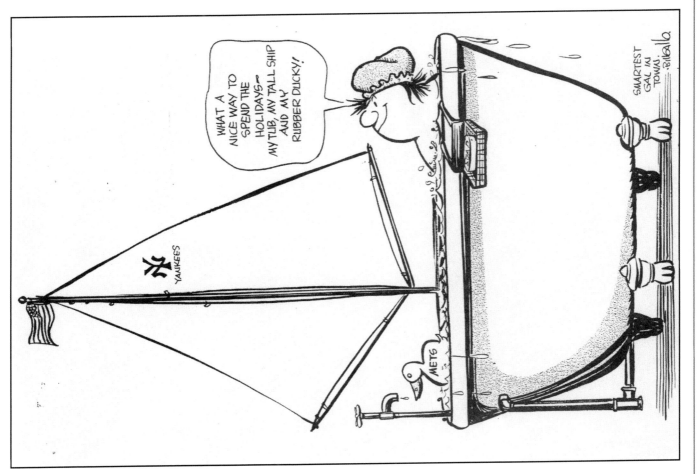

TOP HEAVY

Olympic gold medalist Leon Spinks was a twenty-four-year-old kid with only eight pro bouts under his belt when he won a split decision over a tired Muhammad Ali in February 1978, but the heavyweight crown proved too big for the man. It turned out Ali had just loaned the kid his title; seven months later, in front of 70,000 people in New Orleans, Ali won the rematch. Soon after, Spinks began heading into obscurity.

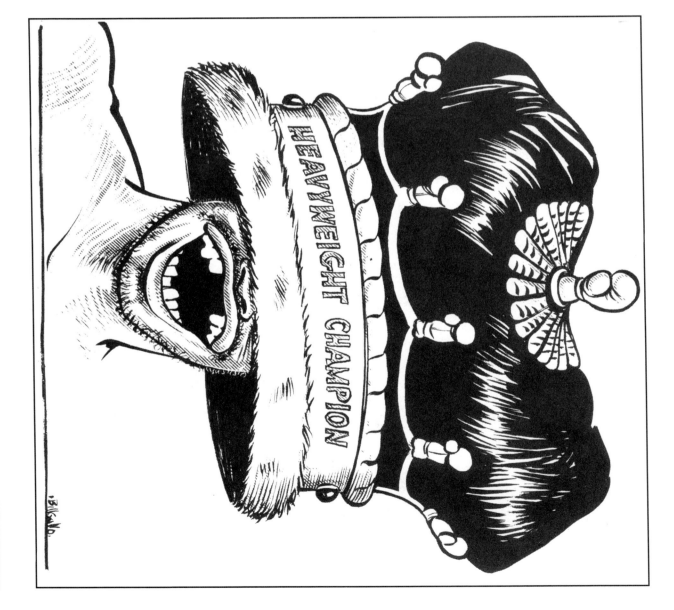

ESCAPE CLAUSE

The winter of 1975–76 saw the demise of the reserve clause, which had allowed a team to lock up a player's services for as long as it liked. Two of the first major leaguers unchained were Andy Messersmith of the Dodgers and the Montreal Expos' Dave McNally, much to the satisfaction of union leader Marvin Miller. This development changed the game of baseball forever.

YOU HOCKEY PUCKS

Hockey is exciting to watch, but what turns me off to the pro game—gets in my way of studying it—is the insistence on fighting. I want to see fighting in a boxing ring; I don't want to see two guys swinging away on ice skates, holding on to one another and trying to stay on their feet. It looks so silly. If you were trying to describe this ridiculous scene to a person who had never seen a hockey fight, the guy wouldn't believe it: "You're crazy! On ice skates?" "Yes, on ice skates."

PLAYING THE FAVORITES

A SHOT OF HIGH DRAMA

Bobby Thomson's pennant-winning home run in 1951 remains a Giant moment in sports history. At first it haunted poor Ralph Branca, the Dodger pitcher who gave up the "Shot Heard 'Round the World." But after a while, much to his credit, he used it.

Ralph is a good guy. What annoys him, and it would annoy me too, is that people talk only about that one pitch—but he was a heck of a good pitcher. He won 21 games in 1947, when he was just twenty-one years old.

THE WINNER OF THIS GAME GOES TO THE WORLD SERIES.... IN THE BOTTOM OF THE 9TH, THE DODGERS LEADING 4 to 1 AND THE GIANTS ARE UP.... DARK SINGLES.... MUELLER SINGLES.... IRVIN MAKES OUT.... LOCKMAN DOUBLES SCORING 1. THE SCORE NOW IS 4-2 (DODGERS)... 1 OUT, 2 MEN ON AND RALPH BRANCA COMES INTO PITCH FOR BROOKLYN...

BOBBY THOMSON COMES TO THE PLATE...

...WITH WILLIE MAYS ON DECK...

...AFTER BRANCA THROWS 1 STRIKE, HE PITCHES TO THOMSON....AND...

BOOM!!! THE SHOT HEARD 'ROUND THE WORLD!'

GIANTS WIN, 5 TO 4.

WHY ME? WHY ME? LEAVE ME ALONE...

THE SCENE LATER, IN THE DODGER CLUBHOUSE.

BRANCA

DRAWING A CROWD

TO HAVE AND HAVE NOT

Ranger fans had to wait fifty-four years between Stanley Cups, and watching the Islanders win four of them in a row in the early '80s didn't improve their mood. I turned that frustration into a rivalry of New York kids. Islander fans gloated over this cartoon, while Ranger fans let me have it good.

HIS CAREER WAS LOOKING UP

Pitcher Fernando Valenzuela always looked up during his windup. What could he be looking at? Ah, ha—we learned that he had his eye on the big prize, the Cy Young Award, and he won it in 1981.

DON'T KICK 'EM WHEN THEY'RE DOWN

Soccer has taken a while to get on a roll—and still really hasn't caught on all the way. This brief history takes us full circle.

A SPOT ON THE BENCH

Although he was not considered a disciplinarian, Casey laid down the law with the Yankees version of the Dead End Kids: Martin, Mantle and Ford.

LINE OF SCRIMMAGE

With the rival American Football League and National Football League set to square off in the Super Bowl, some fundamental differences came into play.

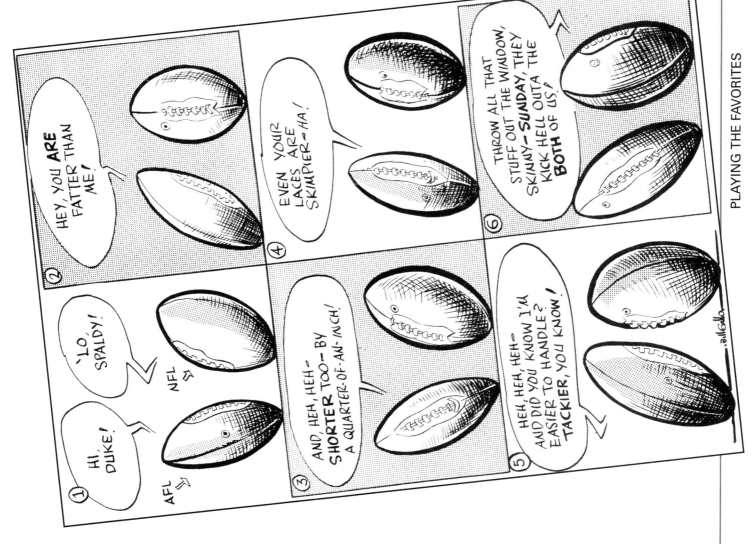

PLAYING THE FAVORITES

WORDS OF WISDOM

In the mid-'80s, Yankees manager Yogi Berra found that you can observe a lot by watching public speakers such as Mario Cuomo and Jesse Jackson.

A FOND FAREWELL

Catfish Hunter was a good guy first and a great pitcher second, and the baseball world mourned both sides of this Hall of Fame pitcher upon his death in 1999.

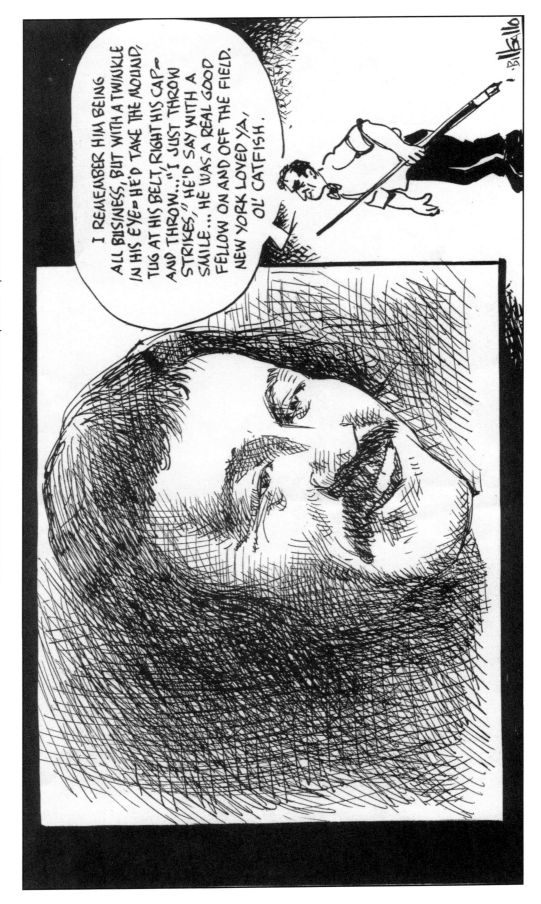

SOMEDAY
HER PRINCE
WILL COME

Basement Bertha is a down-to-earth gal, and quickly found herself on a first-name basis with royalty when Prince Charles visited New York in 1979.

TAPPING A MARKET

In June 1974, the Cleveland Indians tried to boost attendance one night by offering beer for a dime. Drunken fans overran the game and forced a forfeit; the artistic spirit moved me a couple of days later.

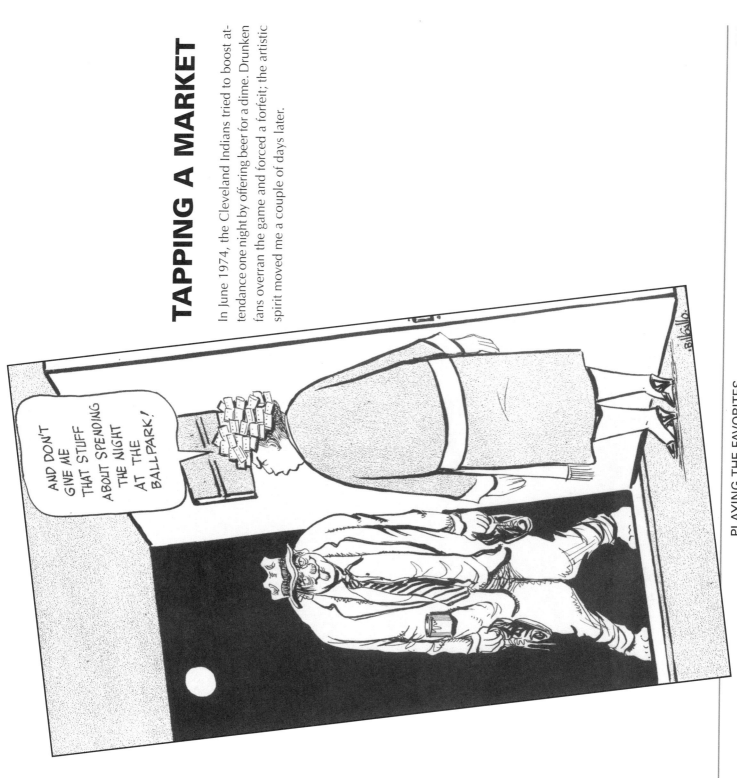

THE BEAST WITHIN

Hockey, particularly when viewed from the upper reaches of Madison Square Garden (aka the blue seats), has been known to have a similarly intoxicating effect on fans. I found a precedent in literature.

BELIEVE IT OR NOT

The Mets enjoyed a great run in 1973, built around the rallying cry, "Ya Gotta Believe." They came up one game short in the World Series against Oakland, however, and Mets skipper Yogi Berra had to make some revisions.

A FINAL SALUTE

In spite of the constant criticism that George Steinbrenner has received since he became owner of the Yankees, he is a vital force in baseball. Von Steingrabber, as I've called him all these years, is a Stirrer and a Doer—he makes things happen. I like Steingrabber, and Steinbrenner, too. The game is richer for having him in it.

Epilogue

IT DOESN'T GET
MUCH BETTER THAN THIS

In this imperfect world, there are times when you look at something and say, "Yes, this is perfection."

It happens to me when I see Fred Astaire dance or hear Frank Sinatra sing. In my mind's eye, I still see Joe DiMaggio play ball and Sugar Ray Robinson in any of his fights, and I say, "Yes, indeed, this *is* perfect."

I marvel at these men and always think this: How could anybody be that good at doing his thing?

Let me add Willard Mullin, the gifted sports cartoonist of the '40s, '50s, '60s and '70s. An unbelievable artist, he was the best I've ever seen in my profession.

While I'm at it, never have I known a better man of letters covering sports than Jimmy Cannon, who regaled New Yorkers for many years. And, don't let me forget my old friend Dick Young, once described by an Associated Press editor as the best baseball writer who ever lived.

Perfect was the right hand Muhammad Ali landed on a weary George Foreman that October night in Zaire . . . Perfect was the way Billy Graham fought Kid Gavilan in the Garden in 1951. Imperfect was the decision handed down. It went to Gavilan, preventing Billy from wearing the welterweight crown.

Perfect is a Milky Way after it's been frozen. Perfect is the groove Ralph Branca put the ball in for Bobby Thomson to hit. . . . Perfect is that cold one that used to wait for me at third base in neighborhood softball games.

Perfect is Rocky Marciano's 49-0 professional boxing record, which may never be broken. . . .

Almost perfect was Man o' War's record.

Perfect is the hour (7:00 P.M.) a bullfight starts in Madrid, the only thing that starts on time in Spain. . . . Perfect was Don Larsen's game against the Dodgers in the 1956 World Series. Perfect was that game David Wells pitched in 1998 and the one David Cone threw the following year.

I can't think of any one punch in boxing history that was as perfect as the left hook Ray Robinson landed on Gene Fullmer in the fifth round to regain the middleweight title. Folks, if you saw that fight in 1957, you were witness to a thing of perfection.

Perfect, too, was Joe Louis knocking out Max Schmeling in the first round at Yankee Stadium in 1938. It told Adolf Hitler what he could do with his so-called super race.

Right on the nose was Joe Namath's guarantee of winning the Super Bowl (over the Baltimore Colts) in 1969.

Perfect was the Rangers winning the Stanley Cup in 1940—and repeating it fifty-four years later, with Mark Messier doing the guaranteeing this time.

Perfect are the shoes that I'm wearing. Whatever color they are, they're proud of it. They take me wherever I want to go without ever complaining. They never hurt my feelings or any of my toes. They never squawk or squeak. And, by golly, if I feel up to it, they sometimes take me dancing.

Perfect is my wife Dolores's paella. . . . Perfect is the feeling you get when visiting the Prado in Madrid and spending two hours looking at Francisco Goya's marvelous paintings. . . . Perfect is rigging a triple fly line and catching a beautiful rainbow trout on your first cast in Phoenicia's wondrous trout streams.

Perfect was the good style and grace of Joe Lapchick . . . and Lou Carnesecca . . . Vince Lombardi . . . Jack Dempsey . . . the wonderful Ray Arcel . . . Wellington Mara . . . Casey Stengel . . . Ralph Branca . . . and Joe DiMaggio, class personified. . . . Joe Louis . . . Muhammad Ali . . . Ed Sullivan . . . Milton Caniff, who drew "Terry and the Pirates" and "Steve Canyon" . . . Rube Goldberg, who was a giant in his profession. . . LeRoy Neiman . . . Weeb Ewbank . . . Jimmy Durante . . . Alice Faye . . . Yogi and The Scooter . . . Rudy Giuliani . . . Tony LoBianco and Danny Aiello . . . Ralph Houk . . . Alexis Arguello . . . Angelo Dundee. These are just a few of the classy people I've been privileged to know.

Perfect is the way I feel at this moment. In my imagination, I see myself standing on a handkerchief and, like Willie Pep or Benny Leonard, not being touched by any foe for a full three minutes. Right now—I mean this second—nobody but nobody can lay a glove on me.

INDEX OF PERSONALITIES